CASE

PHOTOGRAPHIC HISTORY

April Halberstadt

Motorbooks International
Publishers & Wholesalers ®

For my husband HANS,
rugged and dependable,
proven adaptability under a wide range of field conditions
with consistent power at both the belt and the drawbar.
Outstanding among his numerous qualities are
great power for his size and weight,
remarkable ease of handling,
and attractive appearance.

First published in 1995 by Motorbooks International
Publishers & Wholesalers, 729 Prospect Avenue,
PO Box 1, Osceola, WI 54020 USA

Motorbooks International is a certified trademark,
registered with the United States Patent Office

The information in this book is true and complete to the
best of our knowledge. All recommendations are made
without any guarantee on the part of the author or
Publisher, who also disclaim any liability incurred in
connection with the use of this data or specific details

We recognize that some words, model names, and
designations, for example, mentioned herein are the property
of the trademark holder. We use them for identification
purposes only. This is not an official publication

Motorbooks International books are also available at
discounts in bulk quantity for industrial or sales-
promotional use. For details write to Special Sales Manager
at the Publisher's address

Library of Congress Cataloging-in-Publication Data

Halberstadt, April.
    Case photographic history/April Halberstadt.
    p. cm.
    Includes index.
    ISBN 0-7603-0061-5 (pbk.)
    1. Case tractors—History. 2. Case tractors—
    Pictorial works.
I. Title.
TL233.5.H25   1995
629.225—dc20   95-390

On the front cover: When introduced in 1940, the LA was
the largest model of the standard tractor line. It was also a
great seller. This perfectly restored example belongs to
John Black of Slater, Missouri.

On the back cover: A 1924 12-20 crossmotor takes a break
on a sunny day. This beautiful tractor is owned by John
Black and is ready for work or show.

Printed in the United States of America

CONTENTS

ACKNOWLEDGMENTS

This book owes a special debt of gratitude to the generous folks at J. I. Case headquarters in Racine, Wisconsin. Thank you to Case management and staff, especially Dave Rogers, for allowing us to look at the magnificent material in the Case archives. Thanks also to Eldon Brumbaugh and Harry Kline, Case retirees, who are a big part of the Case reputation for engineering excellence.

I am also indebted to those researchers, historians, and other scholars who first tilled these fields; I reaped the results of their labor. So thanks to the journeymen who wrote *the* Case books: Dave Erb, Eldon Brumbaugh, Michael S. Holmes, Randy Leffingwell, Peter LeTourneau, and C. H. Wendel. I really appreciate your scholarship and your affection for the Case corporation.

Thanks again to the many Midwesterners who spent hours positioning their tractors for us. We hope the photographs in this book are worthy of your efforts and your wonderful machines.

Thanks to Mike Dapper, Keith Mathiowetz, and the staff at Motorbooks International for understanding that women also like to be around tractors and other machines that go chugga chugga.

And thanks to John and Libby Hope and Chris and Stephanie Hope for months of Midwestern hospitality while we photographed and researched. Family forbearance and support made this book great fun to do.

FOREWORD

They call this a foreword; that means it is "before the words." Actually, it is a "backwards," a chance to reflect a little about the experience of writing this book and ramble on about why the Case-International Harvester Corporation is so special.

More than one historian has blamed machinery for the disappearance of farms. They say the tractor put men and horses out of work. When the horses disappeared, so did the need to produce millions of tons of hay. It was a double whammy for the farmer.

Other historians prefer the opposite side of the "chicken or the egg" view of history. They argue that mechanization did not cause the disappearance of the farmer; there were already critical farm labor shortages from World War I, and tractors were only filling a need. They point out that the waves of European immigrants arriving in the last part of the nineteenth century needed to be fed, and farm equipment provided relief from the backbreaking drudgery that killed farmers.

Writing this book gave us a chance to do something we always wanted to do—travel around the Great Plains and look at farm life a little differently. We drove around Midwestern America for months. Then, with an image of today's farm fresh in our minds, we went to the Case archives to compare our impressions with the photographs of farm life a century ago.

The Case archives themselves are a special place, a combination library and museum, but better than either. Looking at beautiful scale models of threshers and combines, working models built to be sent to the U. S. Patent Office a century ago, was thrilling. Reading the early advertising brochures and looking at the colorful drawings and sales posters was a reminder of the high level of artistic skill and sophistication behind agricultural sales efforts, skills that the television generation no longer has a chance to see and appreciate.

Working on this book gave us a chance to meet dozens of wonderful folks in Racine and elsewhere, revealing the magnitude of another interesting iceberg we had been admiring. Case equipment collectors are just one part of an enormous group of amateur curators and historians, people who preserve technology out of interest and affection. The best collections of agricultural Americana are not at the Smithsonian; they're in private barns in California, Texas, and the Great Plains...all over America.

The growing numbers of farm machinery collectors and exhibitions are pretty amazing. Tractor pulls and county fair competitions, once a widespread technique for demonstrating and selling agricultural equipment, are now held primarily for entertainment. Demonstrations at the antique equipment shows are not for sissies. There's a real good reason why they call them "iron men."

So we had a unique opportunity to look at the Case corporation and its contribution to American agricultural history. We saw equipment all across America from more than a century ago, much of it still operable. Working on this book allowed us to look at some of the reasons behind the longevity of Case-IH.

CHAPTER 1

BEGINNING OF AN AMERICAN CORPORATION—YANKEE INGENUITY AND THE PIONEER WORK ETHIC

Very few corporations in America have a history that is 150 years old; fewer still are manufacturing companies. The very nature of technological development requires innovation and constant evolution. The ag machinery business was a cutthroat industry despite its pastoral setting.

Consider the overall business environment today. Longevity in any business, especially a manufacturing operation, is pretty rare. In these times of restructuring and hostile corporate buyouts, dozens of proud business names have been obliterated. So when you find a company with a tradition as fine as Case-IH, you can't help but look for the secret to their corporate longevity

and success. It seems that the Case tradition of adapting innovations as they come along is one practice that leads to success.

Agricultural historian Robert C. Williams observes that most farmers in the world, especially the Old World, are traditionalists. They find change threatening and stay with the traditional production techniques that worked for their grandfathers down through the centuries. But in marked contrast, the early American farmers were very adaptable. As Williams says, "To the American farmer, *change* was traditional." J. I. Case typifies the American farmer, open to change, always innovating and adapting.

Business card of J. I. Case Threshing Machine Company. *J. I. Case Archives*

One other thing about the J. I. Case Company. The success of Case, Deering and McCormick, John Deere, and dozens of other shorter-lived agricultural equipment manufacturers is an important part of American history. These are the companies that made America great, the companies that allowed every immigrant to make their own fortunes.

These companies enabled every American to become an entrepreneur. Coupled with the Homestead Act, farm machinery allowed a person to get as big a farm as one could handle. It's the basis of the American Dream, the first step to independence and wealth. And the experience of learning to manage a business, the

experience of thousands of farmers who then applied those lessons to hundreds of other enterprises, is the story of how American corporations developed. The secret of the success and longevity of Case-IH is bound to American values and dreams.

The Not-So-Secret Formula for Case Success

There's a story in the Case company history that says it all... and it may be the not-so-secret Case formula for overwhelming corporate success and longevity. Here's the story that may demonstrate why Case has survived for 150 years.

Here comes the future. A new Model C is chugging over the horizon. Raking in heavy clover—a Model 168 Side Delivery Rake on a Ferguson County farm in Kenosha, Wisconsin, June, 1930. *J. I. Case Archives*

It's a 12 horse-power machine; you can count the noses. The Dingee power sweep is the power unit that provided the muscle for early Case threshers. The steam engines would be a big improvement. *J. I. Case Archives*

Reproduced from an engraving in an 1886 Case catalog, this self-propelled Case steamer with a steering wheel is the machine that gave Case the edge in traction engines. *J. I. Case Archives*

The Raymond engine was manufactured by the J. I. Case Threshing Machine Company under a licensing agreement. You could also buy the smaller models on a rolling platform, moving it around to take care of a number of farm chores such as sawing wood or grinding feed. That made it a portable, stationary engine. *J. I. Case Archives*

Here's Big Abe at work on Highway 65 near Chillicothe, Missouri. This 1913 Case steamer still draws admirers.

J. I. Case built his first thresher in 1842. He worked hard, improved his products, and increased his business. Case innovation and engineering were widely admired, and Case expanded. By 1884, Case had already introduced an improved steam traction engine with the best steering mechanism in the country. It would not be an understatement to say that the Case reputation for engineering excellence was earned in the marketplace and maintained in the field over several decades.

So in 1884, when a farmer in Faribault, Minnesota, was having a little trouble with his new Case separator, he took his guarantee right to the equipment deal-

Ellwood Allnutt says this big steamer has brought in a lot of business over the years. Ellwood has a motel, restaurant, gas station, and an antique vehicle museum, but he's retiring so it's all for sale. This big 1913 Case dates from the golden years of steamers, but J. I. Case Company was still building nearly 2,000 tractors a year when this one was built. Production would continue until 1924.

Old-time power steering. These chains on this steamer control the direction of the front wheels. Response time and maneuverability match the top speed, a blazing 3 mph.

Ellwood says he will part with this one for only $12,500. And his backup steamer, the 1917 Minneapolis, is available too. Steamers are driven by an operator who is standing up; watch that first step!

er in town and complained. But the local service couldn't fix it. Neither could a service engineer from Case company headquarters in Racine. The service engineer was prepared to replace the machine or refund the farmer's money when a terse telegram arrived from Racine. "Am taking the next train. Meet me in Faribault. J. I. C."

The company's founder, Jerome I. Case, had traveled about 400 miles from Racine to southern Minnesota to make good on the Case guarantee. He went to the field, removed his coat and hat, and set to work. After several hours of unsatisfactory tinkering, he asked the farmer for a can of kerosene. Soaking the machine, he lit a match, setting the balky rig blazing. Then he put on his coat and hat and returned to Racine. A new threshing machine was reportedly delivered the next day.

This story has been told over and over again, demonstrating the integrity of J. I. Case and the Case

You can hear it coming. This Case steamer is an annual participant in the show at Hamilton, Missouri.

corporation. But its lessons go a lot deeper. The story appears regularly in Case corporate literature to remind employees about the Case standard for engineering excellence. It is also a reminder that integrity and honor are values publicly demonstrated by the founder and a model for corporate behavior by his employees.

Better than days of employee training sessions, this little story of J. I. Case at Faribault reminds all of us that personal integrity is a corporation's most valuable asset. After more than a century, Case's actions still speak louder than words. It's your customers that keep you in business, not your competition.

Jerome Increase Case; Yankee Ingenuity goes West

When J. I. Case set the thresher on fire in 1884, the J. I. Case Threshing Machine Company had been in business for forty years and was the leading manufacturer of threshing machinery. Case threshers were sold and used throughout America and Europe. Case advertising proudly described the gold medals won by Case machinery.

Historian Michael Holmes says that the best summary of Case's life and beliefs could be summed up in his comments during an interview at the 1876 Philadelphia Exhibition. Case said he built what was "correct in principle and was needed." Case's early advertising said his threshers were "the best available." No doubt about it.

The control panel with all the gauges and the steering wheel. Steamers were not built for either comfort or speed.

The view from the driver's seat on this Case steamer.

The firebox at the operator's foot. At least your feet were warm, winter or summer.

Jerome Increase Case was born in Williamston, New York, in 1819. He went to school and was bright enough to be enrolled in a technical training course at Rensselaer Academy. By age sixteen he was still helping on the family farm but was intrigued by an article he read in a paper called the *Genessee Farmer*, one of the leading agricultural newspapers of that time. The article described the ground hog thresher, and once Jerome and his father had seen it in action, they were impressed. They bought one, and Jerome went into the custom threshing business.

Jerome I. Case went West looking for more opportunity. He took six groundhog threshers, demonstrating and eventually selling five of them. He ended up in Rochester, Wisconsin, a town near Racine, and he had some ideas about modifying the thresher so it would also separate the wheat from the straw.

His developments worked pretty well, and he de-

Rory Esch Finally Gets Steamered

Last summer Rory Esch finally fired up his steamer, and he reports that it was "really exciting." Rory is president of the annual Pioneer Days celebration in Oak Creek and has helped with the old steamers, but this was the first time he was driving a steamer of his very own.

Rory and his friend bought the 50hp Case steamer a couple of years ago and spent the last two years cleaning it up. It was in very good condition. It had been in a garage for about ten years when they acquired it from a woman in Oshkosh. Her husband had been a professor at the University of Wisconsin, Oshkosh, and it had been his pet project. After the professor died, two of his two friends finished restoring it, ran it once to test it, and parked it back in the barn. The steamer had a new set of flues and some patches, and all the major work had been done.

Rory also owns an heirloom 1935 C Case on steel wheels that belonged to his grandfather. His grandfather was one of the founders of the steam show in Oak Creek and had a large collection of tractors. When he finally passed away, his dad, his brother, and Rory picked the Case. When his grandfather had it, the tractor was on all rubber tires. Rory bought some steel wheels for it, and he and his wife hauled it down to the Case collectors show in Iowa during the summer.

Like his grandfather, Rory used to be the kind of collector who was interested in all sorts of equipment. But in the last couple of years he says he has "grown a fondness for the Case company." In part it is because the town of Oak Creek is just about fifteen miles from the Case corporate headquarters in Racine, Wisconsin. But he says that special feeling is also due in great part to his relationship with Case people. They have just been super! And Rory reports that Case guru Harry Kline has been a terrific help with the 50hp steamer.

This is how multi-millionaire J. I. Case got started, working on a thresher crew. The crew is standing on the wagon, pitching shocks of wheat into the thresh-ing machine. The machine separates the straw from the kernel, blowing the straw into a pile and sending the wheat down a chute into a bag.

The Friendly Farmer from Racine. This stacker is an important acces-sory for the thresher, piling up all of the unwanted straw in a neat haystack.

Once a common sight in midwestern summers, a thresher is belted up to a steam-powered traction machine.

Steam tractors hauled the heavy threshers to the field. Then the machines were backed up and belted up to provide power. This was a dangerous operation, since the moving belts needed frequent adjustments and accidents were common.

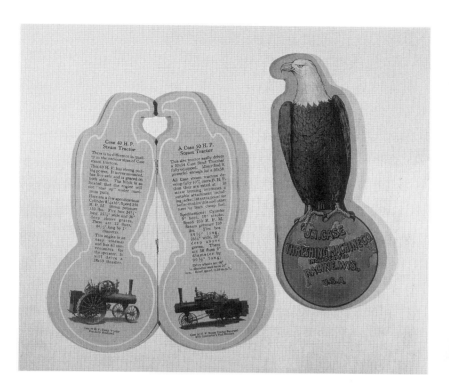

Old Abe, the trademark for Case products, was named for the real bald eagle mascot of the Wisconsin Eighth Company. Old Abe was carried in thirty-eight battles of the Civil War by the Wisconsin volunteers and became an important icon. When Old Abe finally died in 1881, he was stuffed and exhibited around the United States, becoming even more famous. Proudly displayed in the State Capitol Building, Old Abe and his glass case were eventually lost in a fire. *J. I. Case Archives*

Below
The Case thresher pictured on a business envelope. This thresher was built entirely of wood, and the processed grain was delivered out the little chute above the pan on the side. *J. I. Case Archives*

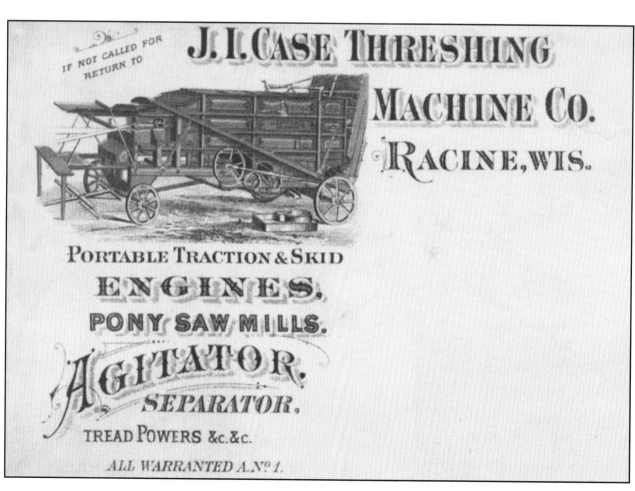

Plowing the hard way—one man, one plow, and a couple of horses. The photograph was taken in 1936 at the height of the Depression and shows just how much work plowing can be. *J. I. Case Archives*

Below
The plows were made with a high yoke and a special bottom to turn this soil, but it's still hard work. The plows are "middle-busters," and the field is near Yazoo City, Mississippi. *J. I. Case Archives*

After plowing comes planting, a time-consuming chore even with a horse, or in this situation, a mule. A Case cotton seed drill in action circa 1931. Seeds are being dropped into the furrow from the can, then soil is folded over with the blade and finally tamped down by the wide rear wheel. *J. I. Case Archives*

A combination binder-harvester made by Case, one of the many important accessory machines manufactured to accompany the threshers. This machine cuts the wheat, bundles it into shocks, binds it with twine, and then lays it on the ground for pickup by the wagon. The twine spool rests inside the container with Old Abe on the side. This machine has been prepared to haul on the road and is pretty clean, although it looks like it has been used for a season or two. *J. I. Case Archives*

Farms ran on horse power and lots of it. Here the horses are cutting and raking their own hay. Tractors would eventually put horses and hay growers out of business. *J. I. Case Archives*

Loading hay with some mechanical assistance. The elevator here is an Emerson-Brantingham No. 5 Cylinder Hay Loader. The Case company bought out the E-B line in 1928, just before the big stock market crash and the Great Depression. *J. I. Case Archives*

Wooden threshers were replaced by steel threshers which were lots lighter and much stronger. This Pea and Bean Thresher can easily be towed by Case trac- tors. The stacker and feeder are folded alongside the body. *J. I. Case Archives*

A Case thresher in action at the steam show in Hamilton, Missouri.

cided to concentrate on building new threshers rather than continue working in the fields as a custom thresherman. He moved his new manufacturing operation to Racine in 1844.

Case Builds His Company on Friendship

The Case Company began with two brothers-in-law and two friends. J. I. Case's threshing machine business was growing and was becoming more than he could handle. When he needed administrative help, he asked someone from his family with some mercantile experience, his brother-in-law Stephen Bull.

The Case company always had a reputation of getting along with others, both family members and business associates. Labor strikes and litigation cost time, money, and emotional energy. Family squabbles have ruined many other corporations. The Case company has been very fortunate that dissension has been relatively minimal.

Looking through the Case archives reveals only a few black clouds. The competition between the Case

Pitching bundles to feed the thresher is slow, hot work. And you need to keep an eye out for any debris that might accidentally get pitched into the machine, like a stray hay fork.

Belting up is an art and a science, a chore for the experienced thresherman.

Plow Works and the Case Threshing Machine Company around 1910 became very difficult for managers, employees, and the citizens of Racine, although for decades the two corporations had coexisted and cooperated. There were also some labor walkouts in the mid-1930s, and a nasty labor strike in 1945 idled workers for 440 days.

A friendly supportive network was an early hallmark of the J. I. Case Company. Being productive depends on teamwork. J. I. Case started out as a thresherman and had a reputation for maintaining good rela-

tions with everyone who worked with him. He carried the lessons he learned as a thresherman into his business practices.

J. I. Case also had an outstanding reputation for fair dealing. Although historical information is limited, it appears that he preferred to buy patent rights or contract for manufacturing rights rather than develop a similar machine that might result in a patent infringement lawsuit. For example, he bought the rights to a "separator" from developer Jacob Wemple and a revolving apron from Hiram Pitts. J.I. Case was always

The original decal and paint job on this vintage thresher.

This thresher and steamer are permanent residents at the county fairgrounds in Hamilton, Missouri, where they make an annual appearance.

The thresher is powered by a steam traction machine, an International Harvester this time. It's a good idea to keep the steamer away from the thresher and the hay wagon. One stray spark could set the entire operation on fire.

interested in mechanical improvements and worked closely with other inventors rather than develop everything by himself. It's a Case business practice that seems to continue; their 1979 joint venture with Cummins Diesel to develop a new engine was probably the most recent demonstration.

J. I. Case had a special ability to develop long-term relationships with other talented mechanics and engineers. One of Case's important friends was W. W. Dingee, a machinery designer who, like Case, was in love with threshers. Dingee held the manufacturing rights to the Geiser thresher, and he wanted J. I. Case to build it. Case and Dingee worked together to improve thresher design and develop the important Dingee-Woodbury sweep.

Case historian Michael Holmes notes that Dingee may have been the person who introduced modern engineering practices to the Case company. While J. I. Case was an experienced field thresherman and a superior mechanic, Dingee had the ability to put the design on paper. Now separators and power sweeps were manufactured from a drawing rather than by copying from a sample part.

A special relationship with another early engineering pioneer, Jesse Walrath, was a factor in building Case steam engine leadership. Case first produced a steam power unit in 1869 and acquired the patent for Walrath's straw-burning boiler. The Walrath patent and the improvements that Jesse Walrath made to im-

The steam tractor operator's viewpoint. The whistle signals starting or stopping work—or a fire!

Threshers need constant repair and adjustment. Where's that baling wire?

The threshing machine can work all day without getting hot, tired, or thirsty. The rest of the crew needs to take off for a lemonade and a siesta.

The Case thresher always draws admirers.

prove the safety and performance of Case engines established the J. I. Case Threshing Machine Company as a world leader in portable steam engines.

The Case Company Picks Up Steam

Steam-powered engines of all types had been used in Europe and America for several decades by the time the first Case steam machine appeared in 1870. Steam power was used for all sorts of enterprises. Like many others, Case saw the possibility of using steam to power threshers.

Case built seventy-five steam engines that first year of 1870, but the customers had mixed feelings. Farmers were very aware of the hazardous boiler explosions and fires from experiences with passing locomotive boilers. Few farmers were experienced boiler-tenders although many farmers eventually became expert.

But the Case Company continued to innovate. A self-propelled steam traction engine, steered by horses, was available in 1878. Steam tractors with steering became available in 1884. And Case manufactured several steam-propelled plowing machines in the late 1880s and early 1890s.

As steam tractors became more popular, they also became lighter, stronger, and more maneuverable. Case developments in clutching and suspension systems helped popularize a machine that was outselling all competitors by the turn of the century. Case improvements led them to pioneer another major industry—construction equipment.

Case may be headlining the "most modern thresher," but their advertising is mindful that many of their customers still farm with horses. *Halberstadt Collection*

The steel thresher was a lot lighter and more portable than traditional Case wooden models. This model has been fitted with rubber tires, allowing the farmer to do custom threshing, thereby recovering some of the cost for this investment. *Halberstadt Collection*

Construction Equipment

Early on, there wasn't much need for road building equipment, because there wasn't much of a need for roads. It wasn't until Henry Ford started mass production of automobiles and John D. Rockefeller started pumping petroleum across America that the need for an all-weather road system really developed. But the Case company was ready with the heavy equipment needed to build roads and highways.

Improvements to the steam traction machines made them suitable for use in road grading. Steam road rollers were available from Case in 1909, and just a year later the Case board of directors voted to expand the line and offer a full range of construction equipment.

Keeping with the Case tradition of acquiring machinery lines, Case contracted with the Perfection Road Machinery Company of Gallion, Ohio, to acquire additional road building equipment. Case bought the entire output of that company, and Case sales brochures began to feature rollers, graders, rock crushers, and other road building equipment.

In an effort to stay abreast of a strong market demand for construction equipment after World War II, Case acquired the American Tractor Corporation (ATC) in 1957. The merger also brought a dynamic executive, Marc B. Rotjman, and a network of industrial equipment dealers to Case. In addition, the merger brought an extraordinary piece of equipment, the first of its kind. It was the loader-backhoe, and it gave Case the edge on all the competition.

Case also acquired another important product in the merger with ATC, the crawler tractor. Case had

Case modified the pea and bean harvester for peanut farmers. Separating peanuts from the vine trash was easier than harvesting tiny wheat kernels. The blower and windstacker for wheat straw have been omitted, so the peanut thresher looks much smaller than a grain thresher with comparable capacity. *Halberstadt Collection*

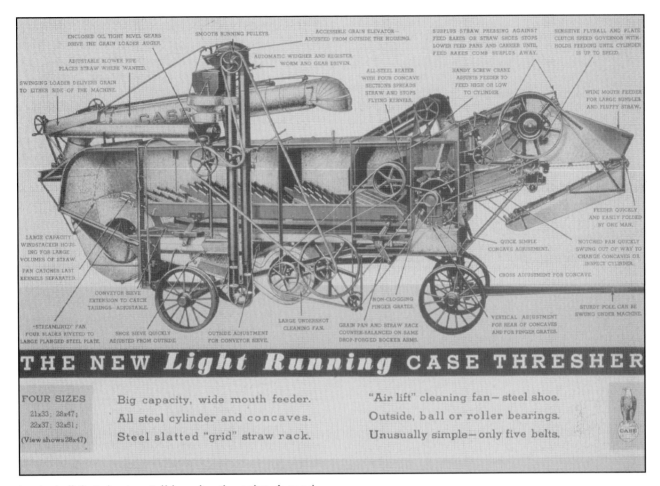

Look at all that sheet metal! Imagine the noise. A good thresherman always kept his ear on how his machine was operating. *Halberstadt Collection*

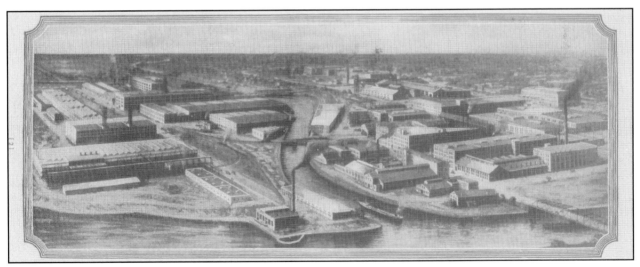

J. I. Case relocated his thresher manufacturing company to the edge of Lake Michigan. This location provided both water and power to operate the plant as well as good access to Great Lakes shipping channels. *J. I. Case Archives*

Branch houses. Regional distributors carried Case equipment as well as implements from local dealers. Many times Case acquired the small, local implement builder and added it to their own line. Note the Foreign Branch Houses listed in World War I. *J. I. Case Archives*

helped pioneer various kinds of construction equipment, but the Case crawler was considered to be just a tractor with treads. At last Case had a heavy-duty machine.

Building the Corporation

As the J. I. Case Threshing Machine Company prospered, many related companies wanted to be included in the Case engineering effort or the Case distribution network. Case dealerships carried a wide range of farm equipment, much of it with the name of another manufacturer. Eventually, Case acquired a wide number of related businesses.

Another key element in Case corporate longevity is the early development of a banking and credit industry. This allowed the farmer to buy one of the huge threshers on credit. The files of the Case archives contain early sales contracts, agreements with farmers to purchase threshers.

Case became very interested in the banking and credit industry, founding the first bank in Racine and setting up a financial network. Although J. I. Case and

The local distributors of the J. I. Case Threshing Machine Company frequently developed their own advertising literature. This little booklet of testimonials was put together by the Nebraska branch house for their customers in Iowa and Nebraska around the turn of the century. *J. I. Case Archives*

This impressive five story brick warehouse in Lincoln, Nebraska, was built in 1893 as a branch house. Dozens of distribution warehouses like this were located in major cities all around the world. *J. I. Case Archives*

Power take-off, old style. With a little steam and a good belt to fit around this flywheel, you could saw lumber, split logs, or thresh grain, but not all at the same time.

Steam tractors weighed in around ten tons and would frequently collapse bridges. Engineers lightened them a little by using drive wheels.

other members of the family served as directors of local banks, Case felt that it was bad business for a manufacturer to lend money directly to customers without proper safeguards. And he felt strongly that a manufacturer should not be in the banking business. The Case Credit Corporation finally came into existence in 1957, at the insistence of their corporate underwriter.

So an important element in Case corporate longevity was the early practice of financing related businesses while remaining at arm's length. Manufacturing plants were kept separate from branch houses; the tractor builders were kept separate from the implement builders, the construction equipment builders, and the thresher manufacture. It was a system that worked really well, most of the time.

But one time it didn't work; it was awful. That's our next story, about the time that J. I. Case set up a new company, put his son in charge, and ended up with a major competing corporation right next door. It was a corporation that lasted for more than fifty years, built quality products with the J. I. Case name stamped proudly on the frame, and ended up in a disagreement that had to be settled by the Wisconsin Supreme Court.

Gasoline tractors were already starting to catch on when this World War I vintage steamer was built.

The Camp Creek Threshers hosted dozens of interesting machines including this 50hp 1916 Case steam tractor owned by the Doehling family.

Can't you tell—it's a Case. The Doehling family from Surprise, Nebraska, put a lot of effort into their restoration.

CHAPTER 2

THE PLOW WORKS—
WHICH CASE PLOW
IS THE REAL CASE PLOW?

Should you stick with the business you know best, or should you branch out into related lines? The Case company did both at different times. And in still another daredevil demonstration of corporate flexibility, Case was even in competition with itself for more than a generation. For Case collectors and agri-

The raised plow, trademark of the J. I. Case Plow Works. For years both the Plow Works and the Threshing Machine Company used Old Abe as a trademark. After a Wisconsin Supreme Court decision, the Plow Works had to come up with a new design. *J. I. Case Archives*

cultural historians who enjoy perverted little quirks of history, it is known as the time when a Case plow was not a Case plow.

How did all this happen? Why were two Racine companies, both founded by J. I. Case, selling duplicate lines of agricultural equipment? Why were both companies using the famous race horse, Jay Eye Cee, in their advertising? How did this strange turn of events get started and how was it finally resolved?

Well, it was all pretty simple and straightforward in the beginning. As a pioneer in the threshing machine business and then a leader in steam traction, the Case company had always been interested in the kinds of implements that farmers were belting up to their steamers. Case himself was a farmer and tested his equipment on his own farm. And he was interested in his neighbors' farm practices, too, always watching for any modifications to equipment that would improve performance.

Plowing was the traditional yardstick used to measure a farmer's ability. Holding and plowing a straight furrow with consistent depth to the end of the field, row after row, was the mark of a real plowman. Plowing was also the steam tractor's biggest and toughest job, the factor which determined how many horses (or how much horsepower) a farmer needed. Plow bottoms that could be drawn cleanly through sticky soils were less strain on the horses. And plows that were easier on the horses were usually easier on tractor horsepower, too.

Case was always looking for ways to demonstrate the field performance of his traction equipment. And

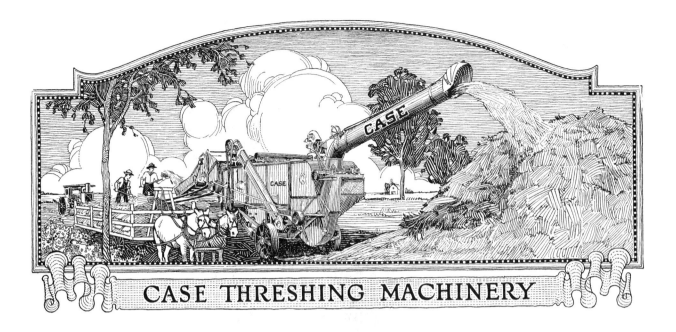

CASE THRESHING MACHINERY

Dale Hartley's Finest Salvage

Dale Hartley owns a terrific RC, and it's been one of his favorite tractors for nearly twenty-five years. Dale acquired this tractor somewhat by chance. He had gone down to a tractor show in Springfield, Missouri, and then wandered over to visit a nearby salvage yard in Parsons, Kansas. In the middle of one of those especially memorable junkyard operations was sitting a little bit of everything, including an RC.

Dale recalls that it originally had a Fordson cultivator on it, which is why it currently appears without a drawbar. Dale acquired it in 1967 for the nice round sum of $100. A friend who had gone to the Springfield tractor show agreed to help bring it home. The new acquisition was hauled back to north Missouri for Dale, gently packed inside a load of hay.

It was pretty rusty when it got back to Kingston. Fortunately, it didn't have to have new pistons, it just needed to be cleaned up. And once it started running, it ran really great. It's not really used for farming anymore, just for shows. It's a regular exhibit at the annual steam engine show in Hamilton, Missouri. Last year it did duty as a power source, hooked up with a belt to run a rock crusher.

Dale Hartley has been involved in the tractor show at Hamilton since its beginning in 1963.

Letterhead and an early catalog from the J. I. Case Plow Works. J. I. Case himself is listed on the letterhead in 1885, along with his son-in-law, Henry Wallis. In just a few years Wallis would take over the company, beginning an enterprise that eventually compete with the Threshing Machine Company. *J. I. Case Archives*

Plowing long perfect furrows, row after row after row, is the mark of an able plow man and the sign of a competent farmer. It's not as easy as it looks, as this exhibition demonstrates. The sulky plow is pulled at the annual Missouri Valley Steam Association show in Boonville, Missouri.

Plowing demonstration; a three-horse hitch pulls an old John Deere single-bottom. That's Andrew, Bud, and Blue doing all the work.

it was pretty apparent that some plow bottoms, that curved metal piece of the plow that cuts and turns the soil, were more suitable for mechanical plowing than others. So when a local Racine plow inventor, Ebenezer Whiting, was looking for a partner to manufacture a new bottom, one that was designed for use with steam traction, the Case family was interested in the investment.

Capitalizing other companies was not a new activity for J. I. Case; he was already involved in many other local enterprises including banking, Great Lakes cargo shipping, municipal improvement, horse racing, and steam traction development. The Threshing Machine Company worked with many smaller suppliers and manufacturers who supplied parts and accessories for their threshers. And if a key supplier ran into a little financial difficulty, the Case family helped by providing loans or additional capital. In some situations they just bought the business.

So a partnership with Ebenezer Whiting and several others to manufacture plows in Racine was a reasonable new venture. The original investors for this Case family venture included Wakely Bull, J. I. Case's brother-in-law, and George Erskine, son of business partner Massena Erskine. Inventor Ebenezer Whiting was actually the only "outsider" in this closely knit family and business partnership.

Whiting had first developed a horse-drawn center draft plow, which also showed great promise as a suitable implement for steam tractors. The new factory for Whiting, Case, and Company was built right next door to the Case threshing machine works. When Whiting left the new company within two years, the firm was reorganized and renamed the J. I. Case Plow Works. Now the investors included partner and brother-in-law Stephen Bull as well as Case's son-in-law, Henry Wallis. So the Plow Works was reborn with the J. I. Case name and an added assortment of

The sulky plow and mixed team.

After the Wisconsin Supreme Court decision, this insert appeared on Threshing Machine Company products, and a similar note was on the equipment catalogs. The companies were connected and affiliated. The Plow Works and the Threshing Machine Company were both founded by J. I. Case. And Wallis was one of Case's sons-in-law. So instead of clearing possible confusion, this little flyer only compounded it. *J. I. Case Archives*

Look for the EAGLE
Our trade-mark

To avoid confusion, the J. I. CASE THRESHING MACHINE COMPANY of Racine, Wisconsin, desires to have it known by all concerned that it is not now, and never has been interested in or in any way connected or affiliated with the J. I. Case Plow Works Company or the Wallis Tractor Company, of Racine, Wisconsin.

35

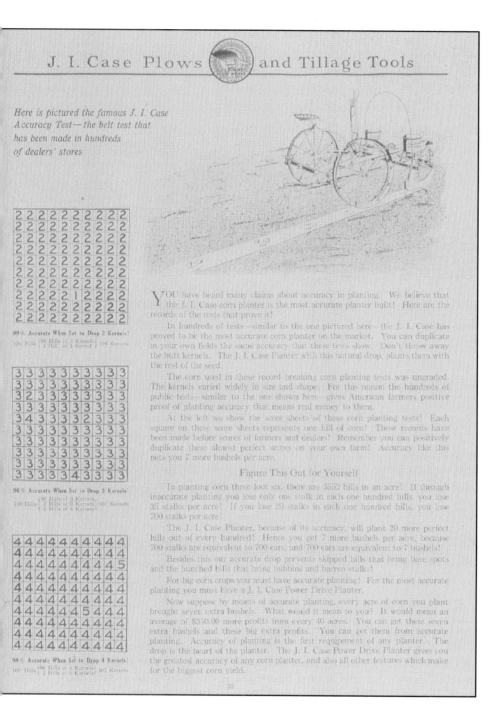

Case relatives in management. The Whiting plows were sold by Case representatives. And the new name, the J. I. Case Plow Works, undoubtedly improved plow sales since the Case reputation for quality was widely known throughout the agricultural industry.

The Plow Works prospered, and after a few years, Case installed his only son, Jackson Case as president. In the beginning, the Case Plow Works worked with the steam traction developers at the Case company.

The firm manufactured plow bottoms and an assortment of other farm equipment designed to complement the steam tractors. But the death of J. I. Case in 1891 brought several changes in the family and in the business.

Death in the immediate family frequently causes the remaining family members to reassess their personal priorities. Jackson decided that he preferred politics to business. His business activities as president of the

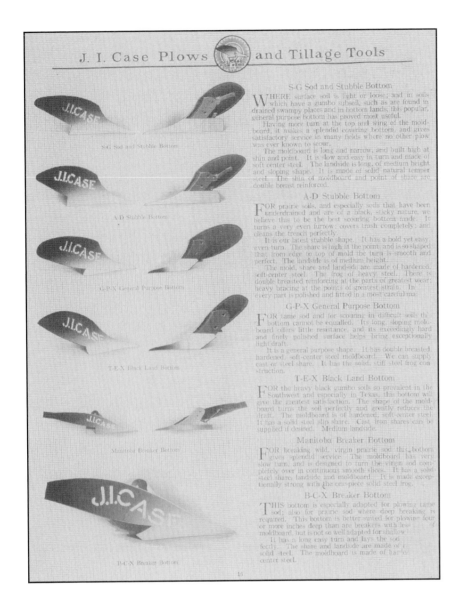

Who's tops in bottoms? Our friends at the Plow Works. Their catalog lists page after page of bottoms and their specifications. *J. I. Case Archives*

Wisconsin Industrial Association and director of the Manufacturer's National Bank prepared him for other responsibilities, and when he was recruited to run for mayor in Racine, he readily accepted the nomination.

The Case family interest in the Plow Works was carried on by Jackson's brother-in-law, Henry Wallis. There were now several dozen family members, all related to the four original partners who depended on the Case companies for their daily bread. Grandchildren and cousins who demonstrated an interest and an aptitude in the family enterprises took their places within the corporate structure. And both the J. I. Case Threshing Machine Company and the J. I. Case Plow Works coexisted happily until the 1890s.

The Rift Appears

The death of patriarch J. I. Case brought several management changes within all the Case corporations and related businesses. Back in the 1860s, there had been four equal partners in the original J. I. Case Threshing Machine Company; Case himself, his brother-in-law Stephen Bull, along with Robert Baker and Massena Erskine. There were originally 10,000 shares divided equally among the four original owners. Case had 2,500 shares of stock to divide among his wife and four children, and he had expressed the desire in his will that his stock remain in the family and that none of the family properties be unnecessarily sold.

But the only son, Jackson Case, was interested in politics and felt that his run for mayor of Racine would eventually take him away from a business career in agricultural manufacturing. He apparently felt that he should consolidate his investments to just the Plow Works holdings. So he reorganized his other Case company stock and directorships and disposed of his Threshing Machine Company stock, concentrating his investments to just the Plow Works. He also sold as much of the other family property and businesses as possible, including the family horse farms. He then ran for mayor, was elected, and began a career in Wisconsin politics.

Partners Massena Erskine and Robert Baker had also passed away, and their stock had also been divided among their families. Of the four original partners, only Stephen Bull remained, with 2,520 shares of stock, by far the largest remaining block. Stephen and his son Frank were still very active in the management of the threshing machine companies and preferred to

concentrate their efforts there, leaving the Plow Works to their cousins. Since they held the largest block of stock, their wishes prevailed. When Jackson Case left the presidency of the Plow Works, his brother-in-law Henry Wallis took the helm. It was a situation that eventually divided the family along corporation lines and caused confusion and social discomfort in Racine for decades.

The 1890s were tough economic times in the United States. There was a major economic depression in America, fueled by speculation in the railroad industry in the late 1880s. The farmers suffered too; so did most businesses. The agricultural equipment industry was no exception, and many manufacturers did not survive. There were hundreds of agricultural equipment manufacturers in the 1890s, and only a few dozen would survive. Both the J. I. Case Threshing

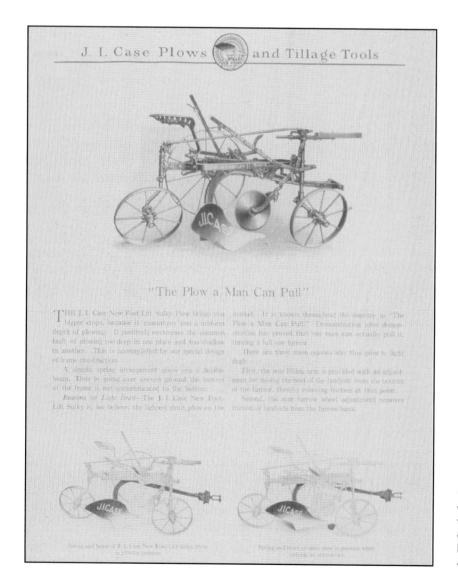

"The Plow a Man Can Pull." Copy-writers have been with us since the very beginning, but the story leads one to believe that this has actually been demonstrated in the field. *J. I. Case Archives*

H. M. Wallis, president of the Plow Works and son-in-law of J. I. Case. In later years, he was much more interested in developing the Wallis tractor, a gasoline machine with a unitized frame. *J. I. Case Archives*

Machine Company and the J. I. Case Plow Works were in serious economic difficulty.

Hard times mean hard decisions, and it soon became apparent that the managers at the Threshing Machine Company were tougher and more capable than their cousins at the Plow Works. Both businesses survived the depression, but the Threshing Machine Company was able to grow in a new and exciting direction while the conservative Plow Works stuck with business as usual. The Plow Works continued to manufacture plows and tillage equipment; the Threshing Machine Company went into building tractors.

The Threshing Machine Company reorganized both their finances and their upper management, demonstrating a dazzling restructuring maneuver that still has audiences amazed a century later. Using smoke, mirrors, and a Milwaukee law firm, Frank Bull and family acquired the Threshing Machine Company, using the assets of the corporation to sell the company to

themselves. It was a bold stroke, but it contributed to the bad feeling between the two companies. Although the reorganization was technically legal, many members of the Case family felt cheated.

The Threshing Machine Company Takes Off

The Threshing Machine Company had sold steam tractors for years, and now an exciting new technology was going to make tractors more available. Dozens of barnyard tinkerers were already experimenting with stationery gasoline engines, trying to fit them onto various wheeled platforms to do dozens of farm jobs. Tiny little one and two cylinder engines were already pumping water, sawing lumber, grinding feed, and helping out with all sorts of chores. More inventive individuals with a spare engine were bolting it to an old wagon, driving a set of wheels. Then they'd run them up and down the county road. Dern fools were scaring the horses!

Engineers at the Threshing Machine Company had been working on both a gasoline tractor and a

Jerome Increase Case, founder of both the Threshing Machine Company and the Plow Works. *J. I. Case Archives*

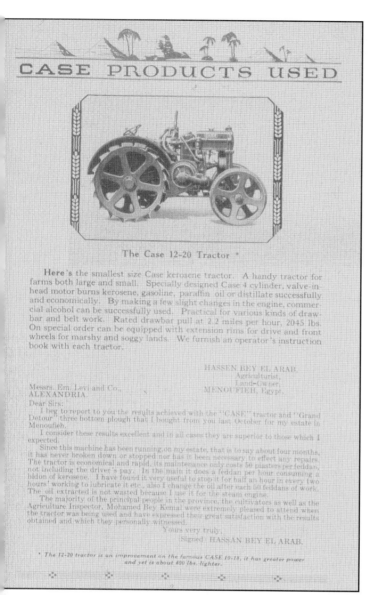

The Case 12-20 Tractor *

Here's the smallest size Case kerosene tractor. A handy tractor for farms both large and small. Specially designed Case 4 cylinder, valve-in-head motor burns kerosene, gasoline, paraffin oil or distillate successfully and economically. By making a few slight changes in the engine, commercial alcohol can be successfully used. Practical for various kinds of draw-bar and belt work. Rated drawbar pull at 2.2 miles per hour, 2045 lbs. On special order can be equipped with extension rims for drive and front wheels for marshy and soggy lands. We furnish an operator's instruction book with each tractor.

HASSEN BEY EL ARAB,
Agriculturist,
Land-Owner,
MENOUFIEH, Egypt.

Messrs. Em. Levi and Co.,
ALEXANDRIA.
Dear Sirs:
I beg to report to you the results achieved with the "CASE" tractor and "Grand Detour" three bottom plough that I bought from you last October for my estate in Menoufieh.
I consider these results excellent and in all cases they are superior to those which I expected.
Since this machine has been running on my estate, that is to say about four months, it has never broken down or stopped nor has it been necessary to effect any repairs. The tractor is economical and rapid, its maintenance only costs 50 piasters per feddan, not including the driver's pay. In the main it does a feddan per hour consuming 2 bidon of kerosene. I have found it very useful to stop it for half an hour in every two hours' working to lubricate it etc., also I change the oil after each 50 feddans of work. The oil extracted is not wasted because I use it for the steam engine.
The majority of the principal people in the province, the cultivators as well as the Agriculture Inspector, Mohamed Bey Kemal were extremely pleased to attend when the tractor was being used and have expressed their great satisfaction with the results obtained and which they personally witnessed.
Yours very truly,
(Signed) HASSAN BEY EL ARAB.

* The 12-20 tractor is an improvement on the famous CASE 10-18, it has greater power and yet is about 400 lbs. lighter.

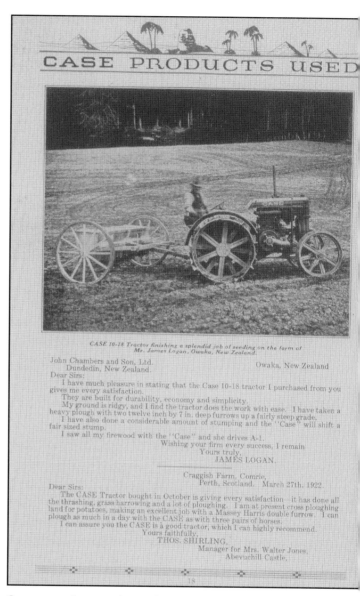

CASE 10-18 Tractor finishing a splendid job of seeding on the farm of Mr. James Logan, Owaka, New Zealand.

John Chambers and Son, Ltd.
Dundedin, New Zealand.   Owaka, New Zealand.
Dear Sirs:
I have much pleasure in stating that the Case 10-18 tractor I purchased from you gives me every satisfaction.
They are built for durability, economy and simplicity.
My ground is ridgy, and I find the tractor does the work with ease. I have taken a heavy plough with two twelve inch by 7 in. deep furrows up a fairly steep grade.
I have also done a considerable amount of stumping and the "Case" will shift a fair sized stump.
I saw all my firewood with the "Case" and she drives A-1.
Wishing your firm every success, I remain
Yours truly
JAMES LOGAN.

Craggish Farm, Comrie,
Perth, Scotland. March 27th, 1922.
Dear Sirs:
The CASE Tractor bought in October is giving every satisfaction—it has done all the thrashing, grass-harrowing and a lot of ploughing. I am at present cross ploughing land for potatoes, making an excellent job with a Massey Harris double furrow. I can plough as much in a day with the CASE as with three pairs of horses.
I can assure you the CASE is a good tractor, which I can highly recommend.
Yours faithfully,
THOS. SHIRLING,
Manager for Mrs. Walter Jones.
Abevichill Castle.

It's a handy little tractor in Egypt, too, according to the happy owner, Hassan Bey El Arab. *J. I. Case Archives*

Case went down under to Australia and New Zealand, but one of their biggest marketplaces was the down-under continent of South America. *J. I. Case Archives*

stationary gas engine during the 1890s and were becoming experienced with the possibilities and limitations of gas power. Case had acquired the patents for stationary gasoline engines for farm use from J. W. Raymond in 1885. Built by Case under a license agreement and known as the Raymond engine, this unit proved to be reliable and efficient.

The Raymond engine was featured in Case catalogs and sold through the Branch houses. The engines were readily accepted and extremely popular, used for a number of applications. For example, the Raymond engines were used to pump water for livestock, reduc-

ing the farmers' dependence on unreliable windmills. Small, self-contained gasoline engines also replaced steam boilers as a power source. And farmers were happy to find a safer, cleaner engine to help out on the farm.

In the early 1890s, Threshing Machine Company management had also contracted with another important inventor, William Paterson of Stockton, California, to help develop a gasoline driven tractor. In 1894, Paterson was given the nod by the Case corporate directors to build a prototype tractor. A successful model was delivered the next year, but persistent problems

Move over, horses! Case crossmotors proved to be just as good for heavy road work as the steam traction engines. This 40-72 is probably showing off a little, hauling six wagons full of material. *J. I. Case Archives*

with an unreliable carburetor made it unsuitable for farm work. Farmers needed a simple machine, easy to adjust or repair in the field. A second prototype also failed to deliver the consistent reliability promised. So the board at the Threshing Machine Company shelved commercial production of a gas-driven tractor for the time being, but this new technology was developing rapidly in other midwestern farmyards and garages.

In the meantime, the tremendous growth in the American population, due to immigration and westward expansion, opened vast areas of the Midwest and West for agricultural development. Competition among farm implement dealers forced many of the major manufacturers still in business after the 1890s depression to become "full-line" dealers for their farm customers. Case was facing stiff competition from International Harvester, John Deere and a host of others. So Case added other related farm equipment to their catalogs and branch office showrooms to encourage farmers to buy from a single establishment. Case sold Raymond engines, Troy wagons, and Grand Detour plows with their other lines of equipment.

By the early 1930's, Case offered graders that were modified versions of the C and L models. *J. I. Case Archives*

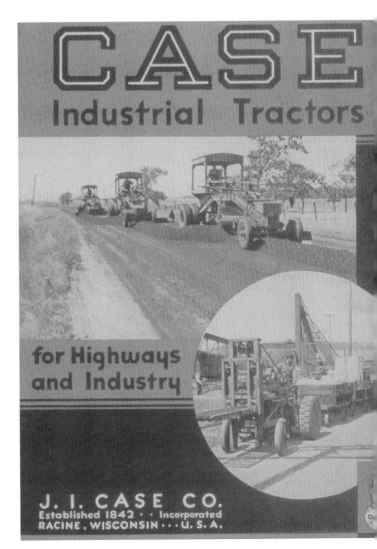

CASE Industrial Tractors for Highways and Industry

J. I. CASE CO.
Established 1842 · · Incorporated
RACINE, WISCONSIN · · · U. S. A.

41

Driving the C with a Bucket of Water

Albert Remme bought his 1930 Model C in 1957 from a Dennison, Minnesota, neighbor who was retiring from farming. He had sold all his equipment, and this was the only piece he had left. "I asked a hundred dollars for it, and they laughed at me," the old farmer said. "So you just go down to the shed and take it." Albert insisted on giving the farmer $100, just in case there might be question of ownership later on.

Albert is not really a Case collector. "All of our tractors have a purpose," he says. His C is no longer used for farming; the Remme's use bigger tractors. But when they want to pull a wagon, or run some errands, they fire up the C. For years the C was his second tractor, and they kept it around because it was very reliable. Even in the winter it would always start right up on the third crank. So it was usually used for chores around the farm.

The old tractor did have a few problems. The elderly neighbor had bought it used, sitting out behind his local tractor dealership. He already had an H Farmall, and it wasn't adequate to run his tillage equipment. So he was looking for a larger tractor, but he didn't want to spend much on it. The dealer first sold him an old 15-30 McCormick, but it used so much oil that he quickly brought it back. Looking around, the dealer offered him a neglected Case, sitting in the back.

The farmer took it home and really liked his old Case. It handled real well and had a low profile. But the cooling system hadn't had proper care. However-er, a little thing like a bad radiator didn't slow the farmer down. He put a ten-gallon can of water at each end of the field when he was plowing. Every time he got to the end of a row, he trickled a little water in his C, and he plowed 160 acres that way every year.

Then in 1957, Albert and his wife acquired the Case and tried plowing with it. The water bucket business was such a chore that the Remme's decided to fix their new old tractor. They took it apart and found that the entire block was filled with sediment, right up to the head. There was no water around the tubes. So they replaced the sleeves, reground the crankshaft, and put in new pistons. They put on a new DC head and manifold and then took it out and went back to work.

It did fine for thirty years or so. Unfortunately, they gave it some antifreeze, and it hurt the rings. So three years ago they took it apart again. The crankshaft and bearings were still beautiful. It got a new set of rings and reground valves. Last summer it was finally repainted.

Albert is very fond of his Case. When he was a kid, his family had a Fordson, but many of his neighbors had 10-20s. They were powerful tractors for their size and were very dependable. He remembers always being impressed by the look of the standard tread tractors with wide fenders. Maybe you could say that owning a Case keeps you young, because it makes you remember your youth.

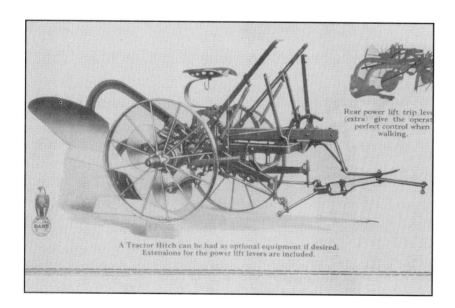

A Tractor Hitch can be had as optional equipment if desired. Extensions for the power lift levers are included.

Rear power lift trip lever (extra) give the operator perfect control when walking.

J. I. Case eventually acquired the right to put the Case name on plows again by buying the ailing J. I. Case Plow Works. This two-way plow is sold by the original Case corporation—Old Abe in the corner says so. *J. I. Case Archives*

The new generation of managers at J. I. Case Threshing Machine Company were an entirely new breed, trained in universities and business schools. They were interested in wider distribution of Case agricultural machinery and sent agents to Europe and South America. Adapting their steam traction technology, Case also developed a line of road building equipment, steam rollers, scrapers, crushers, and graders, equipment that was going to be needed to build streets and highways in a country that was just discovering the automobile.

The J. I. Case Threshing Machine Company was doing very well. The threshing machine business remained strong, and new models were being developed for a wider range of crops; peas and beans, peanuts, clover, as well as the more traditional wheat, oats, and barley. Case had signed a contract with W. R. Grace & Company in 1885 to sell threshers abroad in Chile. There was a branch house in Buenos Aires in 1890 and one in Odessa, Russia, by 1907. The Threshing Machine Company was profitable and looking at tractor manufacture.

The Sattley Plow Turns the Last Straw

While Ebenezer Whiting was developing his plow, other plow inventors across the Ohio Valley and the Midwest were also busy with their own improvements. Over the years, the Case corporation would absorb a number of plow businesses. And one of the most interesting mergers, way down the corporate merger road, would be with the Grand Detour Plow Company of Dixon, Illinois. This was the plow works founded by Leonard Andrus which originally put John Deere in business. But between the 1876 acquisition of Whiting's plow factory and the eventual purchase of Deere's plow works, the Threshing Machine Company was involved with still another plow maker, the Sattley Plow Company.

Even though the Threshing Machine Company was seen as a "full-line" implement dealer, a plow for use with their traction equipment was not offered in the catalogs until 1912. They built a plow to be pulled by their steamers and bought just the plow bottoms, the hardened metal part, from the J. I. Case Plow Works. The Threshing Machine plows were sold separately, to avoid the appearance that they were competing directly with the Plow Works. Talk about confusion in the marketplace!

But as competition between the two companies stiffened, it became pretty apparent that the Threshing Machine Company needed to look elsewhere for plow bottoms. Fortunately, another family member was already in the plow business. Flora Erskine, daughter of

After the turn of the century, the J. I. Case company expanded their world market to more than 100 different countries. They were extremely proud of the international awards and medals and featured them in their advertising brochures. *J. I. Case Archives*

The transition from horses to horsepower took decades, especially on smaller farms. This farmer is using a spike tooth harrow in the mid-20s to break up clods and prepare the soil for planting. There were dozens of tractor manufacturers by then, but he still works the hard way, walking behind the team. *J. I. Case Archives*

We like to think that this is a new middle breaker and lister being tested at the Case company in late 1929. That's the factory in the background with the Case logo on the water tower. *J. I. Case Archives*

The plow man and the photographer have an appreciative audience in 1937, but others whiz by in their autos without stopping. But the outdated wooden plow with a single-bottom suggests that this is a demonstration mule team who is plowing for show, not grow. *J. I. Case Archives*

Below
Cultivating cotton in Grapevine, Texas, in the late spring of 1931. It's the beginning of the Depression years, and several years of bad weather and economic hardship are ahead for these farmers with their mule teams. While many of the farmers farther north wear a jacket and flat cap to work in the fields, these farmers seem to be wearing straw hats and chaps. *J. I. Case Archives*

A Case clod crusher, drawn by a very healthy pair of draft horses near Truesdell, Wisconsin, around 1930. Case implements such as these were so well made that many of them are still in use today, doing the same chores. *J. I. Case Archives*

Below
The famous Emerson-Brantingham gang plow, a masterpiece of balance, easy for horses to pull. Case bought the E-B company in 1928, acquiring the best-selling foot-lift sulky plow. The plows were lifted by the operator's feet, so both hands could stay on the reins. *J. I. Case Archives*

Another essential farm implement for the Case line, this manure spreader was probably acquired by buying another corporation. A team of Percherons is pulling this wagon while the herd keeps an eye on the operation. *J. I. Case Archives*

Another backbreaking chore that could be done with a tractor, spreading mulch to keep moisture in the soil and prevent the topsoil from blowing away. How many wagon loads will it take to cover this field? *J. I. Case Archives*

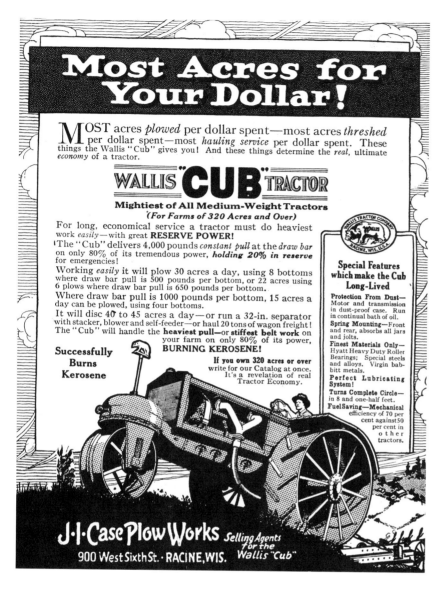

The Wallis Cub pulls uphill in this advertisement from a 1918 farm magazine. This tough little tractor developed by the J. I. Case Plow Works showed real promise, but financial difficulties lay ahead for the Plow Works.

one of the four original partners, had married a fellow who was president of the Sattley company. The Sattley Company manufactured a full line of walking plows and sulky plows. So the catalog of 1913 featured a line called the Case-Sattley plows. But that wasn't satisfactory; the Plow Works wanted exclusive use of the Case name on plows. And their attorney said so. That was the last straw.

The Rift Breaks Open

By the turn of the century noticeable cracks had appeared in the relationships between the two companies. The Threshing Machine Company was doing well, the Plow Works was not as successful. It's not really clear if the rift can be attributed to any one thing, but the trend was noticeable.

Competition in selling plows designed for use with tractors started the trouble, although in the beginning it looked like the two Case companies could co-exist comfortably. The Threshing Machine Company wanted plows for use with the new tractors it was building; the Plow Works was still making walking plows and tillage equipment for use with horses. The two groups seemed to be pretty distinct for quite a while. But some farmers were buying tractors and wanted tillage equipment that could be drawn by either horses or horsepower. And experiments with adapting horse drawn implements for use with tractors was just not working well.

There appears to have been some bad feeling as the result of plow sales competition, but the family seems to have been pretty polite, reluctant to risk con-

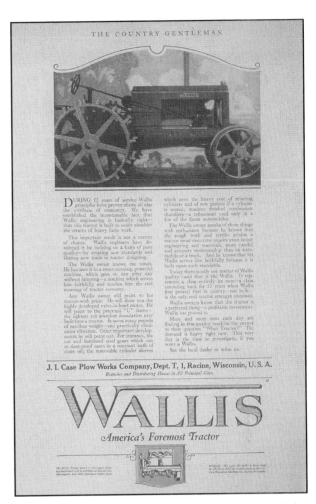

The J. I. Case Plow Works was selling its original line of horse-drawn plows in this 1920 advertisement. Notice all the legal disclaimers and the J I Case name printed on each plow bottom in the picture. The raised arm trademark was the symbol for the Plow Works.

Adding to the confusion, both the Plow Works and the Threshing Machine companies built solid little tractors. The Wallis was sold by the Plow Works through their distributors.

frontation. Even after a lawsuit was filed, people were polite. But it is reported that when the differences caused problems at the Racine Post Office, things could not be politely ignored.

Since J. I. Case and its many related businesses was the largest employer in Racine, mail frequently arrived addressed only to J. I. Case without any additional addressing information. At the same time, litigation was underway in the Wisconsin Supreme Court about the competition in plow manufacture and the ownership of the J. I. Case name and "Old Abe" trademark.

The ruling on the ownership of the J. I. Case name was handed down by the Wisconsin Supreme Court in 1915, and it marked the end of real communication between the two firms. By the time the verdict was handed down, J. I. Case had been dead for nearly twen-

ty-five years, and Jackson Case had been dead for a decade. Although Case's son-in-law Henry Wallis was still listed as the president of the Plow Works, his primary activity seems to have focused on still another corporation, the Wallis Tractor Company in Cleveland, Ohio. The family was clearly going two separate ways.

The lawsuits were resolved in the following way; the J. I. Case Threshing Machine Company could continue to market and manufacture plows and tillage equipment but could not stamp the Case name on the frames. The J. I. Case Plow Works could also market and manufacture plows and tillage equipment, using the Case name. The "Old Abe" trademark went to the original company, and the Plow Works had to design a new symbol. They developed a trademark, a plow held by an upraised arm.

The postal dilemma was resolved by opening all the mail at the Threshing Machine mail room with a Plow Works representative present. As one historian points out, this certainly gave the Threshing Machine managers a tremendous competitive advantage. They got to see correspondence from all the Plow Works' salesmen and customers. The practice ended in 1928 when the Plow Works was finally sold to Massey-Harris.

The Plow Works Gets a Tractor—
The Wallis Cub

Like their cousins, The J. I. Case Plow Works was a full-line implement manufacturer. The gasoline tractor in their line was the Wallis Cub, the first farm tractor built using a unit frame design. The Wallis Tractor line had been developed by Henry M. Wallis, husband of Jessie Case Wallis, one of JIC's daughters. When

Jackson Case left the Plow Works to run for mayor of Racine in 1892, Wallis took his place.

The Wallis Tractor Company of Cleveland, Ohio, produced their first tractor around 1902. It looked like all the other steam traction engines around, a big heavy machine. With the typical Case family practice for acquiring new designs, Wallis acquired a lightweight frame design from Robert Hendrickson, an inventor looking for financial backing. By 1912, H. M. Wallis had an entirely new machine, a light maneuverable tractor on Hendrickson's patented unit frame. The unit frame, frequently called the U-frame, enclosed the engine and transmission.

The unit frame was a very important development in tractor design. It allowed tractors to be a lot lighter, eliminating the heavy frames originally needed to support steam boilers. And most of the moving parts were

The J. I. Case Plow Works sold a line of implements as well as plows and tractors, just like the J. I. Case Threshing Machine Company. This ad appeared after World War I, but most farmers still used horse-drawn planters.

Case Threshing Machine Company advertising from *The Country Gentleman* magazine, June 18, 1921.

now inside the housing away from dirt and weather. The lighter weight was somewhat relative, however. Historian Randy Leffingwell notes that the new Wallis tractor weighed 8,350 pounds, more than four tons of iron. This Hendrickson-to-Wallis-to-Case design was years ahead of a similar Fordson tractor design. Ford frequently gets most of the credit for developing the unit frame.

There was another important engineering refinement as well. It sported a four cylinder engine. Christened the Cub, the Wallis company showed off its performance and reliability by running it from Cleveland, Ohio, to Fremont, Nebraska, a distance of about a thousand miles. The little machine became known as "The Thousand Mile Cub."

Because Wallis was still the nominal president of the Plow Works, Wallis tractors were sold by Plow

The Plow Works advertises its plows in 1919. Notice the J. I. Case name on each bottom. Also notice that the tractor in the illustration looks like a plain vanilla tractor, not a Wallis.

The lawsuit between the J. I. Case Plow Works and the J. I. Case Threshing Machine Company had just been settled in 1920, so Old Abe reminds Threshing Machine Company customers in the February issue of *The Country Gentleman* that the original Case corporation had been around since 1842.

Works salesmen, and the Cub factory was finally moved to Racine in 1919. But the J. I. Case Plow Works continued to have financial difficulty. Massey-Harris, a Canadian agricultural manufacturer, bought the whole shebang in 1928, acquiring the J. I. Case Plow Works, the Wallis tractors, and the rights to the Case name. The Wallis tractor name was eventually folded into the Massey-Harris line, disappearing around 1938. But Massey offered the J. I. Case name for sale, back to the parent Threshing Machine Company. So in 1928, the merger of the Plow Works and the Threshing Machine Company was acknowledged with a corporate name change in the parent company. Coming full circle, the company was known once again as the J. I. Case Company.

So which Case plow is a genuine Case plow? Both companies were founded by J. I. Case, and both sold first quality plows and tillage equipment. Both companies were managed by descendants of the original Case families and their partners. Both companies had headquarters in Racine, Wisconsin.

Other plow builders who distributed their tillage equipment through Case branch houses kept their names proudly on their equipment, sometimes alongside the Case name; Sattley, Grand Detour, and the Emerson-Brantingham foot-lift plows. The answer is that they can all legitimately claim to be Case plows, if they say "Case" anywhere on the frame. And expect to pay extra, if you can find one for sale...they're still worth it.

Copywriters at the Plow Works were just as convincing as the staff at the Threshing Machine Company. This ad featuring Case implements was printed in the same February 1920 issue of *The Country Gentleman*.

A reversible plow, an extremely useful but lethal-looking tool, allows the plowman to throw a furrow either way. The plow pictured was sold in the late '30s, a product of the J. I. Case Company. *J. I. Case Archives*

CHAPTER 3

TRACTOR DEVELOPMENT—
WHAT'S HOT IN RACINE?

Now in order to tell you the next part of the story, the part where Case also becomes rich and successful as a leader in the tractor business, we also need to step back a little and take a look at power farming around the turn of the century. Steam traction on the farm was now a tremendously

The old and the new. This Case steamer is running circles around the two little Flambeaus in a demonstration at Boonville, Missouri. Case made steam engines until 1924, the first Flambeau Red tractors appeared in 1939.

successful technology, and Case had made a fortune with their steam product line. They were the market leaders, outselling all the competition.

Beginning in the Middle

Telling the story of the development of Case farm tractors means that you start in the middle, after the corporation had already been an international agricultural industry leader for seventy years. It must have been simple to make a million dollars in the tractor business...just start with a million or two from the threshing machine business. But Case was not in a hurry to get into the gasoline tractor business. They had already been the leader in steam traction for more than thirty years, and they weren't about to jump on Old Number 1 and ride off in all directions. Agricultural equipment manufacturers, like farmers, have the reputation of being very conservative.

Maybe that conservative "wait and see" attitude comes from the very nature of farming. Dependent on the weather and wary of pests and disease, the farmer has enough to worry about without having to think about his equipment. Farming is a little like planning a picnic, says one farmer. "We try to get everything ready," he says, "and then we wait and see what the weather is like that day." And farm equipment manufacturers, dependent upon the success or failure of crops, tend to be even more conservative than their farm customers.

At the time, back around the turn of the century, Case was not sure it wanted to get into the tractor business. For one thing, there were too many ama-

CASE KEROSENE TRACTORS

teurs. Every other barnyard mechanic was fooling with putting a little 2 or 3hp stationary engine on a wagon. Many small museums today have one of these prototypes in their collection, built by talented local mechanics who solved some of the problems of a gas engine driving a wagon. And then there were dozens of automobile builders who were jumping into tractor production.

Besides the amateurs, there was some pretty stiff competition from a couple of smart, college-trained agricultural engineers who were pioneering the tractor industry. Charles Hart and Charles Parr not only put a working tractor in the field as early as 1902, the Hart-Parr Company sales manager, W. H. Williams, usually gets the credit in the history books for coining the word "tractor." By 1907, the Hart-Parr factory in Charles City, Iowa, had sold about 600 gasoline tractors.

Even by 1910 there were only a total of about a thousand or so tractors on American farms, and a good number of them were still Case steamers. Most of the rest of them were made by Hart-Parr. Their best selling "Old Reliable" 30-60 came chugging along in 1907. But off in the distance, Henry Ford, the inventor who was making automobiles cheap and accessible, was itching to get into the tractor business.

Ford was born on a farm, hated the drudgery, and had a working prototype tractor in 1907. He wanted to get into the tractor business, but the board of directors of the Ford Motor Company wouldn't let him. Frustrated, he went outside of his auto company and started a whole new enterprise to build tractors.

The first Fordsons showed up around 1918 and

The 20-40 and it's big brother the 30-60 looked like steam engines. There was a reason; Case was using the same frame. The canopy on the 20-40 extends nearly the entire length of the machine. *J. I. Case Archives*

This looks more like a tractor; the 12-25 arrives in 1913. *J. I. Case Archives*

soon became as popular as Henry's Model T; now tractor competition was really tough. Case was not a leader in gasoline tractors, and now the market was dominated by the Fordson, the Farmall, and scores of smaller tractor builders. Why would any successful company want to take on more competition?

Case entered the tractor industry through a different door than most of the other manufacturers. Case was already building heavy steam traction engines and wanted to offer the farmer another power option for the big field traction machines. They were going for size, trying to build a big gasoline engine, one with enough horsepower to handle the chores and still pow-

er the heavy chassis of their steam machines.

Most of the other builders were imitating a motor car; fitting a small horsepower stationary engine onto a light frame to replace the horse. Eventually they were going to meet in the middle. Case tractors got smaller and lighter, and the rest of them got a little bigger. But it wasn't until the mid-1920s that they all got together in the middle of the room.

It's interesting to note that Case-IH, an international leader in tractors and implements, did not pioneer gasoline tractor technology or develop an implement line...it acquired both of them. And when we hear about Case's relative status as number three or

It sure looks like a 12-25 is in there under all that rust.

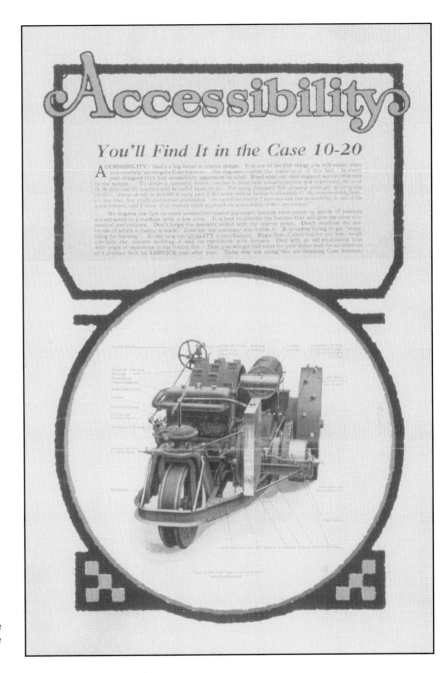

The fourth member of the first Case tractor quartet is the 10-20, a little tricycle. *J. I. Case Archives*

four or five in tractor sales, depending on what year we're comparing, it's important to keep The Big Picture in mind. Tractors were a sideline for Case, not the big enchilada.

Sometimes it's a little difficult for Case owners at the antique tractor shows when the competition brags that their tractors were more popular or more widespread. During the early development competition of the gasoline tractor, the Threshing Machine Company was busy building and selling threshing equipment and a line of heavy industrial equipment, steam rollers,

and graders. And they were selling threshers all over the world; in South America, in Europe, even in Russia! So being number three or four or five in tractors alongside leadership in threshers is still pretty impressive. Case owners have learned to smile tolerantly and respond quietly, "Well, you're right," they say. "Case tractors really don't appeal to just...anybody."

Case was a relative latecomer to the gasoline tractor race. As a leader in threshers and steam engines, they stuck with their proven winner and continued to sell steam traction. Company records show that about

Case experimented with a cultivator tractor before World War I. The horses may be out to pasture, but they are still on the farm. *J. I. Case Archives*

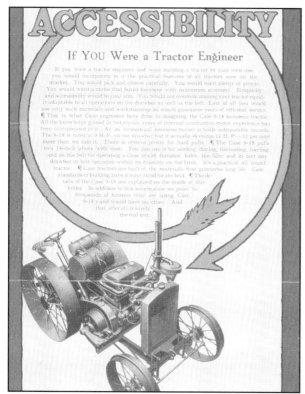

24,000 steam tractors were built after 1900. But gasoline tractor manufacturing plants were springing up all over the midwest; one source lists more than 200 of them by the end of the 1920s. Automobiles with gasoline engines were catching on; so were tractors. The first gasoline tractor built by Case showed up nearly a decade behind the pioneering Hart-Parr machine.

Case had been experimenting with gasoline engines off and on for twenty years. They had marketed a stationary gasoline engine, the Raymond engine, in the mid-1890s. And their first contract with inventor William Paterson to build a gasoline-powered traction

The 9-18 and the 10-20 are the first of a new Case line, the crossmotors. These tractors had their engines mounted crossways. This 9-18 is the four-wheeler; the 10-20 was a tricycle version, an important forerunner of future tractor development. *J. I. Case Archives*

It's got four wheels, so it's the 9-18.

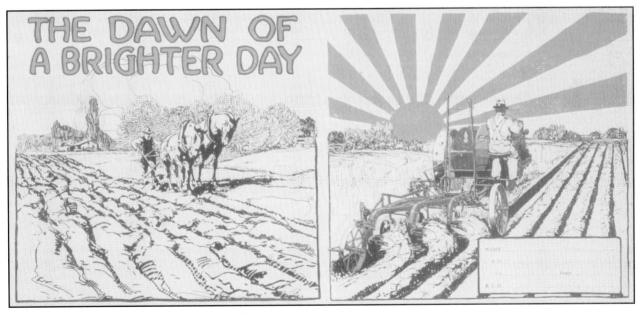

The tricycle crossmotors promised the Dawn of a Brighter Day. Finally, a small, maneuverable tractor. The single front wheel was helpful in cultivation. *J. I. Case Archives*

The 10-18 went everywhere, even to Europe to help out and win awards. *J. I. Case Archives*

engine was in 1892. Maybe their entry into the marketplace was delayed because they lost a key engineer, David P. Davies. Davies left Case in 1897 and did not return until 1910.

By 1911, Case was finally ready to debut their first gasoline tractor. You could say that Case was slow to get into the gasoline tractor race. Maybe you could say that Case wanted to maintain their reputation, offering only high quality equipment. Or you could say that Case was just "over-engineering" again, building a gasoline tractor consistent with all the rest of their equipment. No matter what the reason for the late arrival, the bugs were worked out before any new Case machine went into production. Old J.I. Case himself would have been proud. It was another machine built to his standards, the most perfect manner possible.

Model 60; the First Gasoline Tractor in 1911

It had a lot of resemblance to the steam tractor. That's no surprise... it makes sense to stick with a successful design, and so the early Case gasoline tractors looked just like the Case steam tractors. The early de-

The 10-18 showed up during World War I, and Case called it the "baby." But they also said it was so handy around the farm that you really needed two of them. *J. I. Case Archives*

The crossmotors get a distinctive profile starting with the 12-20. The slanted exhaust pipe means this tractor has an airwasher. *J. I. Case Archives*

Coming up the hill, a 12-20 starts plowing in this 1926 picture. The small wheel on the left helps keep the furrows straight. *J. I. Case Archives*

Below
The 12-20 was rated for three bottoms, 12hp on the drawbar. The long handles make it easier to adjust from the driver's seat. *J. I. Case Archives*

The crossmotor line-up. The 15-27 and 22-40 were about as big as the farmer wanted to go. *J. I. Case Archives*

The biggest crossmotor, the 40-72. It's too big for most farms, but it's just right for grading roads. *J. I. Case Archives*

This big crossmotor sports a calliope whistle, one of the benefits of owning a tractor with this kinky exhaust system. *J. I. Case Archives*

The 15-17 was an all-round machine. This one is shown coming up the hill with a Tractor Guide, a long pole which helps keep furrows parallel. *J. I. Case Archives*

signs substituted a gasoline engine for a steam engine using nearly the same chassis. The newest addition to the Case traction line weighed in at over twelve tons and could run on nearly anything available. Farmers were used to firing up the boilers on the steamers with whatever they had available—wood, coal, or straw. The Model 60, or 30-60 as it was called, could run on a variety of petroleum fuels. The farmer could run it on gasoline, or start it with gasoline and then switch over to kerosene or some other low grade distillate.

The first gasoline tractor came equipped with a massive belt pulley mounted on the side of the engine. Belt pulleys on Case steam tractors had been used for years to power threshers. This new model was designed to fit right in with the other equipment in the field and not scare the horses or the farmer. The frame was also massive, designed by engineers who were used to providing support for steam boilers.

Despite the size, it seemed to sell, 125 the first year and another 294 units the second year. It provided a lot of power and was rated at 60hp, although Case

The calliope whistle on this 22-40 looks like a fire hose. Case sold whistles as an accessory; this one chimes three tones.

promoted it at 75hp. It provided 30hp at the drawbar and was actually a lot more power than the average farmer really needed. And the Case reputation cost plenty, $2,500. Of course they gave a 5 percent discount for cash.

Little Brother Arrives—the 20-40

Seeing the need for a smaller machine, Case quickly followed production of the giant 30-60 with the much lighter, cheaper, and subsequently much more popular Model 20-40. Introduced a year later, little brother quickly outsold the larger machine. It sold 796 units when it was introduced in 1912 and a whopping 1,173 units the following year.

It provided 20hp at the drawbar, 40hp on the engine, and weighed a relatively petite seven tons. It was designed for the same jobs, powering a stationary

You can spot a crossmotor a mile away. Just look at that nose!

This derelict 12-20 is part of a museum collection.

This 12-20 Case crossmotor belongs to John S. Black of Slater, Missouri. The protrusion on the side is the characteristic crossmotor.

thresher and hauling a heavy load. But it was smaller and less expensive, priced at around $2,000, within the financial reach of a few more farmers.

Not only was the new kid cuter and more popular, it turned out to be an award winner as well. It won a gold medal in its class when exhibited at the annual Agricultural Motor Competition in Winnipeg in 1912. It continued to test well in the Nebraska Tractor Tests, recording higher performance ratings than the advertised 20-40. It was durable and reliable and very popular with farmers who needed to pull five or six bottoms across the prairie.

Two More Additions, 12-25 and 10-20

Quick to spot a trend, and watching the competition out of the corner of its eye, Case brought out two even smaller traction engines in 1913 and 1914. Automobiles were selling very well, and rural Americans were very interested in gasoline-powered vehicles.

The 12-25 and 10-20 were designed to appeal to

John Black's 12-20 is probably nicer than when it left the Case factory. Did they ever pinstripe the frames in Racine?

No detail is too small. John Black's 12-20 even has the maintenance instructions carefully outlined.

John S. Black's 12-20 crossmotor is more nicely restored than most automobiles.

This 18-32 industrial was acquired by the Iowa Highway Commission in 1928. The exhaust pipe has been modified, pointing down in front of the rear wheel. Hopefully, this keeps the bad air out of that snazzy cab, definitely an aftermarket addition. *J. I. Case Archives*

For those enthusiasts who prefer their crossmotors on steel, Dennis Ficken brought his 12-20 to the Boonville show.

the small farmer, someone who was using a three or four bottom plow. The American gasoline tractor market was developing very quickly, and now the small farmer had a number of options. The Case 12-25 matched the Bull Tractor Company's offering, also rated about 12-25. The most popular tractor offered in 1914, "The Bull with the Pull," was the tractor to beat.

The following year Case brought out still another model to match the competition. The 10-20 was the smallest and cheapest tractor in the Case line, directly competing with a new machine built by the Bull Tractor Company, known as the Little Bull. Built as a three-wheeler, the Case machine cost twice as much as Little Bull. But Case reliability and reputation for quality prevailed over the underpowered Little Bull.

Case advertisement for the new "L," the tractor that made the Case reputation for tractors. *J. I. Case Archives*

Below
New power for a new age. Cutaway drawing shows the chain drive. Developed by David P. Davies, it was the transmission that made a Case virtually indestructible. *J. I. Case Archives*

John Richmond's Case 1935 Model L

John Richmond works for the U. S. Department of Agriculture's Soil Conservation Service and patrols a rural beat in northwestern Missouri and eastern Kansas. While traveling near Elwood, Kansas, a few years ago, John noticed the rusting hulk of an old Model L standing alongside the road and stopped to investigate. John had restored two other tractors previously, but neither were Cases. But the L had an irresistible appeal; "I liked the looks of it—and the fact that it was so big," he said. "And I have always been interested in the 'wheatland' type tractors with the wide front ends. So I had already decided I wanted one of that type."

The owner was a casual Case collector who had picked up the relic out in the western part of the state, brought it home but hadn't proceeded much further with the restoration project than to get it off the low-boy. The engine was rusted solid, there was water in the transmission, and a few minor components—like a piston and cylinder sleeve—seemed to be missing. Concrete had been poured in the rear tires for additional traction, a pretty common practice in parts of Kansas. But an offer of $300 induced the owner to part with the L, and John collected the beast and brought it back to his little tractor hospital at home.

The first problem was to find the missing components. Some turned up in the previous owner's shop; others had to be purchased.

Next came the problem of the rusted-up engine. "Everybody has their own secret potion for loosening up rusted parts," John says, "but the main thing is a lot of patience—and a big block of wood and a hammer!" John's magic elixir is a combination of diesel fuel and a rust remover sold by John Deere.

The engine was overhauled while still in the tractor. The Case L has large inspection plates in the block, allowing access to the crankshaft bearings, rods, and pistons from below. John worked on one cylinder at a time, usually working on just one cylinder each session.

Once the old pistons were loosened and the crank could be turned, it was time to order new pistons and rings. Despite the age of the machine, both pistons and rings were available by special order from a local auto parts store. "Things weren't as hard to find as you'd think," John said. "There was still a listing for the Case Model L in the auto parts catalogue, so I was able to get the rings that way. And the local International dealer still had a set of original pistons that had been on the shelf for a long time but that were available for purchase. Some parts had to come from a dealership in Arkansas, where the L was especially popular and where spares were particularly plentiful. One cylinder sleeve had to be machined, but the other three needed only polishing; with the new pistons and rings installed (and after a run-in period), compression is excellent."

The project took a year of intermittent effort, with assistance from John's father and a local mechanic. Finally, with everything in place, it was time to fire up the old L for the first time. With the machine in gear, the spark advance set at "start," and the throttle cracked, John towed the resurrected L with another tractor—and it fired right up. "We pulled it around the driveway a few times and it took right off," John reports. "It was a really exciting day. With just a few adjustments to the valves, it ran like new!"

John takes the L to tractor shows in northern Missouri and occasionally rakes hay with it. He's used it for some plowing, more for the fun of it rather than as a working machine. "It feels like it has all kinds of power," he says. "It is a little bit slower than a modern tractor, and it needs quite a bit more room to turn at the end of the field—but it has a nice solid feel, as if you could do just about anything with it! It uses about three to four gallons of fuel an hour if you're pushing it—quite a bit of gasoline."

"The tires have been replaced, but the rims were original. It had an umbrella stand on it when we got it, but we have removed it."

The 10-20 sold reasonably well despite the heftier price tag of nearly $900.

The heftier price tag was due in part to a bigger engine. This is Case's first real design with a four cylinder engine. The lighter tricycle design and bigger engine gave this tractor plenty of pull and a lot of maneuverability. Well, it was more nimble than the rest of the tractors the farmers had been driving.

At the time there were also a few other major manufacturers with a tricycle; Allis-Chalmers, Massey-Harris, and a number of others. The tricycle design was quickly phased out in favor of a machine with four wheels. But the single wheel in front had proven quite useful, especially for cultivation. The small, single front wheel arrangement was an important and extremely useful feature. It has been used in tractor design since

The L and C together, shown on rubber tires, but painted a dull gray. *J. I. Case Archives*

As long as we're experimenting with tires, let's try something really wild. This Model CI has been fitted with airplane rims and tires. *J. I. Case Archives*

The L features a PTO in the rear, suitable for operating a binder. This farmer is cutting about eight miles northwest of Rockford, Wisconsin, in 1930. *J. I. Case Archives*

that time, usually offered as an option on a row crop machine.

However, the tractor market was rushing ahead, faster and faster. World War I was drawing to a close in 1918, and the farm boys had seen Paree. Some of them were returning to the family farm, and it was clear that they were ready to use modern equipment. The automobile was catching on, and now Henry Ford had a few ideas about designing and selling farm equipment to farmers.

International Harvester was introducing a very useful feature on their tractors, a power take-off drive shaft on the back that could be used to operate a binder. Waterloo Boy had developed a tractor with a distinctive two cylinder "pop-pop" engine, a machine so attractive that John Deere & Company bought the entire company. The famous Johnny Popper had arrived! The Fordson and the Farmall also showed up in the field in 1918, sleek, attractive, and trim machines that performed well. Case had its work cut out.

The Crossmotors—1914

Case had always been considered a conservative company, but even conservative companies like to make a lot of money and have a big piece of the market. Case was quick to realize that gasoline traction engines needed to give the farmer a lot more than just horsepower to drag plows around a field. Farmers needed a machine that could be belted up to power a thresher—a reliable machine that was relatively simple to operate.

Other tractor builders were coming out with machines that were modifications of the automobile, lightweight but cheap. Following the trends in the rest of the tractor market, engineer David P. Davies was directed to use a smaller motor. The Case company had 100 or so extra automobile engines in stock for two years, and this looked like a good way to use them. The auto engines may have been stockpiled for another Case venture, automobile manufacture. Case was also building cars in Racine, from about 1910 to about 1925. So in 1914, the J.I. Case Threshing Machine

Company's board of directors gave Davies permission to go ahead and build a smaller tractor.

The 10-20, The Four-Cylinder Answer

Case's engineering response to all of the slender, airy looking machines in the field was to provide a solid looking, tough little bulldog of a tractor. And performance was important. Again the Case reputation for "over-engineering" resulted in a reliable machine that was tough enough to stand up to Midwestern winters. And Case made one more important engineering decision, one that would set them apart from the pop-pop's; they decided to go with a four cylinder engine.

Tractor competition was fierce. Every backyard mechanic with an automobile was tinkering, adapting it to farm use. And talk about inventive! One historian notes that there were more than a dozen kits to modify the family's Model T Ford for farm use. And every other mechanic with a few extra bucks seemed to be opening a tractor manufacturing plant. The number of tractors on American farms went from 17,000 in 1914 to 37,000 just two years later. The number more than doubled again in another two years; over 80,000 tractors were on farms in 1918 at the end of World War I. The Case reputation was holding the door...but the rest of the pack was definitely having an impact.

By 1919, there were so many tractors on the market that farmers were having a tough time picking a good tractor. Since many farmers had gotten stuck with unreliable or unsafe machines, the state of Nebraska

Meet the family, starting with big, powerful L, handsome, clean cut C, and the two little specials. *J. I. Case Archives*

No job too wild for a Case plow to handle. This plow is planting forest trees as part of a federal reforestation program in northern Wisconsin. *J. I. Case Archives*

The model CC was the first tractor that combined a cultivator and plowing tractor. This CC is powering a combine, harvesting oats which were flattened in a windstorm. *J. I. Case Archives*

How to start an L—and keep your thumb out of the way. This one had a mouse nest that had to be relocated first.

enacted some legislation. Starting in 1919, any tractor sold within the state of Nebraska had to pass a few performance tests.

Confident of their tractor's performance, Case was one of the first manufacturers to haul their machines to the test track in Lincoln on the campus of the University of Nebraska. Case tractors tested comfortably above their advertised ratings. So now Case marketing proudly included Nebraska Tractor Test scores alongside all the international Gold Medals.

Two new designs from Case engineering were recorded as Tractor Test No. 3 and Tractor Test No. 4 at the Lincoln track. The new crossmotor Case Model 10-18 was the first Case machine tested, followed by one of the biggest selling of the early Case tractors, the 15-27. And for the first time, the Case implement

Who needs fancy pressure gauges? The oil pan on the L had two little holes, one above the other. If you remove the screw from the top hole, and oil leaks out, you're still good to go. If you take the screw out of the bottom hole and nothing drains out, you're in trouble.

Drive along the back county roads in northern Missouri, and you might see one of these. It looks like an original owner Case Model L, sitting there in the shed, just waiting to be adopted. The owner of this machine, however, is pretty wily. The most fun he gets these days is having some unsuspecting fool turn into his driveway, hoping the old man is willing to dicker.

catalog pictured a tractor on the cover. Power farming had arrived at Case.

There is something very appealing about the boxy appearance of the little crossmotor, known as "X-motor" to its friends. This tractor is here to work! And the jaunty angle of the exhaust is a distinctive signature. This is the machine that firmly established Case as *in* the gasoline tractor business. But why put the motor crossways?

There were several good reasons, all driven by engineering considerations. Crossmounting allowed Case to install a fully enclosed, simple and efficient, two-speed transmission with straight-spur gearing. The transverse crankshaft provided a straightforward design with a minimum of moving parts. That made it easy for a novice mechanic, or a farmer, to understand and repair this machine. Threshers and other auxiliary attachments could be run directly off the end of the crankshaft, accessible on the left side of the tractor. And putting the engine squarely in the middle balanced the weight of the machine; the competition was already in trouble with tractors that rolled.

They don't even look like they belong in the same family. The square, solid, beefy L makes the RC look pretty runty by comparison.

Dale Hartley is the county commissioner in Buchanan County, Missouri, and he keeps his Case RC (row crop) on its original steel wheels.

The 15-27 and the Airwasher

When the 15-27 was introduced in 1919, it quickly became a best seller and set the path for Case design for nearly a decade. It had a four cylinder engine (remember the John Deere only had two cylinders) and a couple of additional features that improved reliability, an airwasher and a unique intake manifold. These features give the X-motor its signature, the jaunty exhaust pipe.

Dust and chaff in the carburetor intake could now be minimized, important to farmers working in dirty conditions. The air intake manifold was provided with a water-filled canister, part of a complex system that allowed only clean air into the carburetor. The air was not only clean, it was also pre-warmed. Exhaust gases from all four cylinders were routed around the intake manifold, warming the intake air and improving fuel economy. Those Wisconsin winters can be pretty tough; Case was designing tractors that would match their owners.

The unique manifold system provided the opportunity for another special feature, a whistle. Case had provided tractors to work at nearby Baraboo, Wisconsin, home of the circus. Historian Michael Holmes notes that Case sold a steam traction machine named "Hercules" to Ringling Brothers in 1892 for use in their parades. Now some farmers took a lesson from the circus folks at Baraboo, installing calliope whistles on their exhausts. The whistle had been an important feature of the steam tractors, signaling the start and end of a work day and alerting the crew in case of fire. Now the gasoline tractors could sport one too. Case sold whistles as an accessory item.

The crossmotor was a solid tractor design, but the farm economy turned sour in 1920, the first year of production. Fortunately, Case had a strong company and a solid reputation with the models it had produced during World War I. The economy recovered slowly, but it was several years before tractor production rose to the 1919 level.

Even though the 1920s are generally seen as a decade of booming prosperity and economic growth in America, a closer look shows that the farm economy was slow to recover. Investor and consumer attention were focused on auto development. In addition, the number of tractor manufacturers grew, as many mechanics with a little capital decided that tractor production and auto production were almost the same. By 1929, there were nearly 200 tractor manufacturers. Case was trying to compete in a slow market with a lot more competition.

Virtually no other major manufacturer was still producing a crossmotor; they had all moved on with newer technology. Case still had a wide line of X-motors, eight sizes with additional attachments to suit every purpose. There were machines outfitted to work in orchards, machines for rice fields, and machines set up for road construction. Steel wheels were standard, but you could get cast iron, rubber, and an assortment of lugs and cleats to provide better traction. Case offered rubber tires on its models as early as 1919.

Crossmotor Accessories

Two important additional features were introduced on the crossmotors: a power take-off (PTO) and a tractor guide, a device which allowed the operator to plow a straight furrow with a machine. Case had a solid line of tractors, offering various sizes and options for different farm conditions and pocketbooks. But things were not going to get any easier for Case. Although there would be a new president at Case in 1924, International would bring out the all-new Farmall that year, and John Deere's Model D was already extremely popular.

Introduced in 1936, the RC was the only tractor Case brought out during the Depression. However, the smaller frame and single front wheel made it an extremely valuable tool for row crop farmers.

Keeping kids interested in farm chores was always a concern. Some of the early sales brochures state that buying a new tractor is one of the best ways to maintain enthusiasm. A new Case Model C was just the ticket. *J. I. Case Archives*

Standard and Row Crop Tractors 1929–1940
The Model L Appears.

Leon Clausen had a few new ideas about tractor design. That is, of course, one of the reasons Case recruited him, bringing him from John Deere in Illinois to Case headquarters in Wisconsin. There were a few refinements made to the crossmotor line after Clausen arrived, but only a few. A remark made by Clausen, which appears in the Erb-Brumbaugh corporate history, really sums it up. "When I came to Racine, Case's tractor line was obsolete, both in appearance and performance." After Clausen arrived in 1924, he focused the research and development at Case on building a replacement for the X-motors.

Better carburetion, reliable starters, and smoother transmissions were available on automobiles, and farmers expected these improvements on their tractors as well. Case was ready just in time, introducing the new Model L in 1929 and the companion Model C a little later in the same year. Both models were extensively tested by Case company engineers and then by a select group of farmers. Both models were in the marketplace and doing very well before the economic downturn of the 1930s.

Understanding the need for a row crop tractor, the engineers first modified the Model C into a C-Cultivator, known as the CC. It is usually identified by the widely adjustable wheels, easily adapted to a variety of crops. *J. I. Case Archives*

The salesmen told the Case engineers that a two-row cultivator with a very high clearance was needed, so the Model CC was modified to become the CCS, sold as the "sugar cane" tractor. Asparagus farmers liked it too. *J. I. Case Archives*

A pretty and popular tractor, the RC introduced the chicken roost steering arm across the top. This attractive RC belongs to John Richmond.

John Richmond goes off into the sunset on his RC.

Competition didn't get any easier. First there was the Depression to deal with, then there were all the mechanical improvements that were spurred by the automobile industry. Farmers were pretty demanding customers. Performance, reliability, safety, and price were all important criteria, and there were a lot of tractors on the market.

A 1929 farm equipment catalog published by the *Implement and Tractor Trade Journal* lists dozens of tractors contributing to the farmers purchasing dilemma. Advance-Rumely offered the Oilpull and the Do-All. Cletrac and Caterpillar had tractors that ran on tracks. John Deere, McCormick-Deering, and Hart-Parr had a range of models. And then there were all of the smaller, more regional builders offering tractors especially suited to local conditions. Builders like the

A restyled Model RC arrived in 1939. With a redesigned grille, a four-speed transmission, and the new Flambeau Red paint job, it looks like a new machine. This hot number belongs to Dennis Ficken in Boonville, Missouri.

Model R got a restyled grille and paint treatment too. Here it is on standard treads with the original paint, part of Dennis Ficken's collection of 40 Case machines.

Finally, Case goes aerodynamic with totally new styling underneath the Flambeau paint. The farmers loved the tractors, but reaction to the paint was mixed. It faded fast and looked too much like the paint scheme on Brand X. Most agreed, however, that it was an enormous improvement over the Depression gray. *J. I. Case Archives*

The Model L, modified to the LA, was the most popular tractor Case produced. It was produced for nearly twenty-five years and with a little more than 50hp was the perfect size for a larger farm. It was noted for smooth belt power for threshing and lumbering chores. This solid machine has been outfitted with a calliope whistle, because even a hardworking LA wants to have a little fun. *J. I. Case Archives*

Starting the L

The Model L uses the original self-starting system—a crank that you turn yourself. Even with a well worn-in engine, this is not an exercise for wimps. Here's how you do it:

Ensure that the transmission is in *neutral;* if the tractor starts in gear, it can easily run right over the person turning the crank.

Open the fuel shut-off valve (normally turned off after shut-down) to provide gas to the carb.

Open the throttle (push *forward* on the Case, unlike many other tractors) about two notches.

Set the spark advance lever for the magneto to *start;* this will prevent kick-back on the crank (a notorious source of broken arms in the past).

Set the choke; first prime the engine by cranking once or twice with choke closed, then open the choke to start.

Crank the engine, beginning with the crank at the bottom, "six o'clock" position, and pull up about a quarter turn—keep your thumb on the *outside* of the crank (a notorious source of broken thumbs in the past); after three or four tries, it ought to fire and run.

"If the weather is cool and the oil is cold, it is just about impossible to crank," John says. "In the past, folks used to drain the oil and coolant to bring inside to keep warm overnight. Some built fires under the engines, to warm them, and it was common to heat radiator water, too, in order to get the engine warm enough to start in cold weather. They didn't have any antifreeze at the time. Starting a fire under your tractor must have been very dangerous, but people had to get their chores done."

A nicely restored Model SC, the smaller version of the D. This one still maintained the steering configuration from the earlier models.

Two important exhibits from Dennis Ficken's collection, the R and RC. These were important transition tractors, the last of the Depression era machines. The new grille styling and paint foretells a Flambeau future.

Looking like a daddy longlegs, this Model SC-3 has a front axle that really reaches over the row crops. Another one of Dennis Ficken's pets.

Twin City Company in Minnesota, Huber Company in Ohio, and Mead-Morrison from New York.

There are somewhat conflicting stories about Leon Clausen's sensitivity to farmers' needs. On one hand, there are memos and notes showing that when the sales force asked for newer, more appealing tractors Clausen responded, "Don't listen to what they want! Just tell 'em what you have to sell." On the other hand, there is a lot of evidence that shows that the new Model L and the companion Model C incorporated every feature the competition sported and a few more.

The materials were tested, the assemblies were tested, and the finished machines were tested. Prototypes were reportedly released quietly in California for field tests. The Erb-Brumbaugh history states that about ninety prototype Model L tractors were left in California, sold to farmers who had participated in the testing.

When Case had the bugs worked out, they took the tractors to Texas for more open field testing. The results were carefully noted, and a few more refinements were made. The Model L was featured in an advertisement that compared it with the Model 20-40 of a decade earlier. "Your tractor dollar is twice as big today as it was 10 years ago..." screams the headline.

Case advertising made the most of the improvements. Posters compared the new Model L with the 20-40 from a decade earlier. "Costs half as much and does nearly twice as much work in a day..." claimed the copywriter. The new model had three speeds; the old one had two. The new model offered power at three points: belt, drawbar, and PTO, compared with two on the old model. The old model sold for $2500, and the new one cost about half that price. Satisfied customers quickly validated the claims. Over 16,500 units sold before the end of 1931, nearly 7,000 the first year alone.

The Model L pioneered some other features which made it more attractive to general farmers. It had more clearance under the axles, keeping crops from being crushed. It was the first Case tractor with a unitized design, although the Wallis tractors and the Fordsons pioneered the concept. It featured the oil-bath air cleaner designed by Case, an enormous benefit to farmers in dusty conditions. And the Model L pioneered a tough, chain and sprocket final drive, a design so reliable that it remained on Case tractors until the 1950s.

The Model L was the big brother in this little family, showing up with wide shoulders at a rated 40hp. It ran on kerosene or gasoline and could pull three or four plows under usual conditions. Model C was smaller but virtually identical with a four cylinder engine, three-speed transmission, and roller chain drive, coming in at about 27hp. Both machines were modified as new improvements were shown to improve performance. Rubber tires were offered in 1934, and electric start options were made available when they showed up in the marketplace.

The new styling paid attention to the details.

Even the gas cap got aerodynamic styling.

Always attentive to detail, John Black's LA even has an authentic Mason jar. That's so you can tell this is a real working tractor, not just another pretty face.

Left
Here comes John Black on his beautifully restored LA, one of the most popular tractors that Case ever built. John says that the first tractor he ever drove was an LA.

Outstanding in its field, the Case Model LA was the biggest model of the standard tractor line—and the biggest seller.

Handsome, Clean Cut, Powerful—the Model C

Model C came out almost at the same time as the bigger Model L, and it is nearly identical. Side by side, the only difference is one of scale. But the scale was a critical factor, because it was pretty apparent that, in order to be competitive, Case would need a general purpose tractor, one that could be used for cultivation. And the Model L was just too dern big!

Now the advertising shop at Case poured on the adjectives. This was the tractor that offered everything.

"In all sorts of situations, Case tractors successfully cut costs in every way. They furnish low cost power. They give loyal and dependable service. They show the stamina and endurance needed to get the jobs done day in and day out, season after season."

It's hard to tell here whether we're talking about a tractor or a horse. A tractor can be known for its reliability, but loyalty and stamina? The brochure described

All the bells and whistles. The Case 400 has a diesel engine, a new transmission, and a new paint job.

A surrey with the fringe on top—the new 400.

A hardworking industrial tractor, a DI in original condition with Dennis Ficken driving.

Dennis says this DI is on original rubber, and he should know. He's the tire distributor for this part of Missouri.

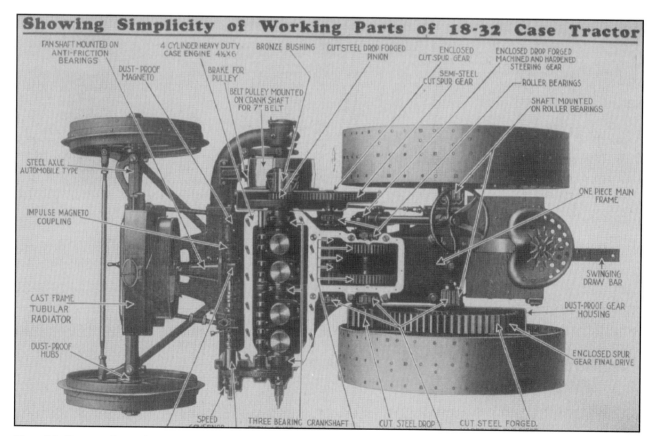

Showing Simplicity of Working Parts of 18-32 Case Tractor

FAN SHAFT MOUNTED ON ANTI-FRICTION BEARINGS

4 CYLINDER HEAVY DUTY CASE ENGINE 4⅛x6

BRONZE BUSHING

CUT STEEL DROP FORGED PINION

ENCLOSED CUT SPUR GEAR

ENCLOSED DROP FORGED MACHINED AND HARDENED STEERING GEAR

DUST-PROOF MAGNETO

BRAKE FOR PULLEY

SEMI-STEEL CUT SPUR GEAR

ROLLER BEARINGS

BELT PULLEY MOUNTED ON CRANK SHAFT FOR 7" BELT

SHAFT MOUNTED ON ROLLER BEARINGS

STEEL AXLE AUTOMOBILE TYPE

ONE PIECE MAIN FRAME

IMPULSE MAGNETO COUPLING

SWINGING DRAW BAR

CAST FRAME TUBULAR RADIATOR

DUST-PROOF GEAR HOUSING

DUST-PROOF HUBS

ENCLOSED SPUR GEAR FINAL DRIVE

SPEED GOVERNOR

THREE BEARING CRANKSHAFT

CUT STEEL DROP

CUT STEEL FORGED

It's a bird's eye view of an 18-32. That is if you're a bird with X-ray vision. The insides of a Case look just like the outside, solid and straightforward. *J. I. Case Archives*

The "tractor wars" are just heating up in 1916 when this ad appeared in *The Country Gentleman*, the "oldest agricultural journal in the world." The competition was pretty tough when the Hart-Parr and the Bull were the machines to beat. *Halberstadt Collection*

this little machine as "handsome, clean cut, and powerful!" This tractor sounds so wonderful you might let your daughter marry one.

The Model C could be configured all sorts of ways for all kinds of farm work. You could get optional equipment for orchard or row crop work. Model CC came as a tricycle with the front wheel available with either one or two tires. It could be configured for working vineyards or for cultivating lettuce.

Then there were all sorts of sporty extras you could buy after you selected the basic configuration. You could opt for seat cushions, a canopy, odometer, front and rear bumpers—the options were limited only by your pocketbook. One of the sales brochures lists some of the reasons to rush out and buy a new Case.

"Operator can sit on a spring seat or stand comfortably on large, roomy platform."

"The hand-operated clutch makes the Case tractor safe even for a small boy to drive. There is no danger of the Case hand-operated clutch slipping into engagement when the tractor should be standing still."

Some say that Model C also stands for "chicken roost," a long steering arm mechanism that gives the Model C as distinctive a profile as the jaunty exhaust pipe on the Case crossmotor. The popular tricycle option on the Model C led to the development of the smaller Model R, a 17hp machine designed for general farm use. It too had a chicken roost along the top although later models dropped the steering shaft to one side. Introduced at the height of the Depression in

This advertisement from *The Country Gentleman* from June 1918 does not mention the war in Europe. The fact that Case is taking out a full-page ad is as interesting as the ad contents.

1935, sales figures show it sold over 17,000 units in its six years of production. It was almost as popular as the larger Model C which had taken nearly twice as long, twelve years, to sell about 20,000 tractors.

The Cultivator—Model CC

Way back during the crossmotor days, Case had toyed with the idea of building a powered cultivator, a device that looked a lot like a tractor with a row of teeth permanently fastened between the wheels. The early prototypes looked very fragile compared with other Case equipment, and the experiment was abandoned until the mid-1930s. The Model C, a four wheel tractor, was built specifically with cultivation in mind. Now designer Davies rebuilt the front wheel to

a "gooseneck," allowing both a higher crop clearance and letting the tractor fit neatly between rows. This refinement was labeled the "CC." The Model CC could be modified further for very high crops, and there was even an extra special Model CCS for sugar cane.

By the mid-1930s, Case engineers had also worked out an implement lifter known as a Motor Lift. This allowed power from the engine to be used to raise and lower implements, especially useful for turning at the end of a row. It is the feature that made the Model C and the CC an especially useful and extremely popular tractor.

Mindful of the flexibility and popularity of this general purpose tractor, Case decided to design a special group of implements just for the Model CC. This

One of the early gasoline tractors, a Case 12-25, being hauled by a Case company truck about 1917. Both the tractor and the truck are equipped with steel wheels. Since the wheels on this 12-25 show a fair amount of good Wisconsin farmland on the treads, we might assume that this tractor has just come back from a test run. *J. I. Case Archives*

special package included the four implements most often used on a small farm: plows, cultivators, seed drills, and a simple mower.

The Row Crops—R and RC

Case was able to remain competitive during the Depression years by limiting the number of models offered and by bringing out only one new tractor, the Model R, midway through the decade. But the R offered all the engineering improvements and agricultural features a farmer needed at a reasonable price. It represented a new mindset at Case engineering, the focus toward providing equipment specifically for the small farm market.

Case had started out in the thresher business, working with grain farmers who had large acreage and needed big machines. Rural America had changed, and now Case business was beginning to focus on a new customer, the farmer with less than 100 acres—the farmer who practiced mixed farming. This customer usually grew some corn or other row crop and raised a few head of cattle or pigs.

The Model R (and RC) represent, a very important transition tractor for Case. It was designed to compete with a similar small tractor built by Farmall, the F-12. The Model R started out with a lot of the features of the earlier C tractors, such as the chicken roost steering shaft, but the steering was later modified to match the CC. It started out with a three-speed transmission, like the C, and then got a four-speed. And the later models got the benefit of some of the new grille styling and the hot red-orange Flambeau paint that the engineers were testing for the new series.

The later Model R and RC are special because production was so limited during its five-year life span. Only a few thousand models were built, and this little tractor came in only three varieties: the standard, a row-crop, and an orchard tractor. At a rated 17hp with a turning radius of about 7ft, this is the little tractor you can use to mow the lawn. But the little RC prepared the market for the next Case tractors, the Flambeaus.

KEROSENE — CASE — TRACTORS

The Handiest Tractor Of Them All

THIS Case 9–18 Kerosene Tractor includes all those practical and handy features that farmers most desire in a small tractor.

This 3400 pound tractor pulls two 14-inch plows anywhere a good team can continuously pull one 12-inch plow. It delivers 33⅓% more drawbar horsepower than rated.

While light in weight, it is built according to Case standards of sturdiness. It weighs but little more than a team of horses.

It has a 4-cylinder Case valve-in-head motor and burns kerosene successfully and economically. An efficient air washer prevents dust and grit entering the cylinders. An improved cooling system includes pump circulation and Sylphon Thermostat control. In dozens of ways this tractor is far in advance. It is the pattern which others try to follow.

In plowing, all wheels run on the unplowed ground. Its all-steel gears are enclosed and run in oil. There are six Hyatt Roller Bearings for gear box, bull pinion shaft and rear axle.

This powerful little tractor, the most efficient in its class, can drive a Case 20x28 Thresher, fully equipped; a Case No. 12 Silo Filler; Case 17x22 Hay Baler and other machines requiring similar power.

No other small tractor offers you so much. When you buy it, you are obtaining the utmost.

Before you buy, investigate the Case 9–18. A Case dealer will be glad to tell you all about it. Or write to us direct.

J. I. Case Threshing Machine Company, Inc.
(Founded 1842) 1261 Erie Street, Racine, Wis., U. S. A.
(739)

"It weighs but little more than a team of horses." This small, lightweight kerosene tractor was a popular model in 1918.

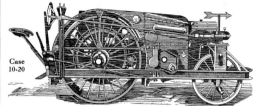

Case 10-20

Not Merely for Plowing

The Case 10-20 Tractor is adapted for all kinds of farm work. It pulls manure spreaders, harrows, planters, hay tools, harvesters, road-scrapers, etc. It will drive silo-fillers, threshers, balers, feed-mills, lime pulverizers and do many other belt jobs.

The Product of 75 Years' Experience

Because of this long experience in the manufacture of farm implements it is natural that Case products represent values that cannot be duplicated. The Case 10-20 weighs only 4800 lbs.—much less than other tractors of equal capacity. It has a four-cylinder Case-made motor which our experience has proved absolutely essential in any light tractor. The Case 10-20 Tractor is designed with utmost simplicity and freedom from complicated parts. All parts of the motor are easily accessible, so no dismantling is necessary for any adjustment.

Designed and Built in Case Shops

Every Case tractor is designed and built by Case-trained workmen, right in Case shops. It is not bought piece by piece outside and assembled. This includes our specially designed tractor motor. We *know* that Case tractors represent the best that experience, money, time and modern machinery can produce. That's why *every* Case product is backed by an absolute guarantee to perform as well, or better, than any other product of its kind.

All Case Products Lead

Case steam engines, Case threshing machines, Case road machinery are all leaders in their own field. Each one offers the utmost at a reasonable price, performance, reliability and service.

Write today for our complete Case catalog. It is an album of information that should be on the table in every farm sitting room. It is beautifully printed, with many interesting scenes and reproductions in color.

J. I. Case T. M. Co., Inc., 270 Erie St., Racine, Wis.
Founded 1842

There are five sizes of Case Tractors — the 9-18, 10-20, 12-25, 20-40, 30-60. A size for every farm.

Write TODAY for more information about the Case 10-20 Tractor or whatever size you need.

The unique Case 10-20, the first successful three-wheeled tractor, especially suited to row crops. The arrow mounted above the front wheel allowed the operator to steer accurately. It would be twenty years before the next row crop tractor design.

This Case Model C is not a stripped-down version without fenders and tall exhaust stack. Case offered a CI and LI for industrial and road maintenance work.

Looking at the soil on the front wheels and grimy condition, this tractor has just come back from serious work. *J. I. Case Archives*

Case Thinks about Diesels (1933)— for about Five Minutes

The Depression years of the 1930s also brought another interesting tractor development, diesel power. The railroads were using diesels with great savings in fuel and manpower. Steam-powered equipment, threshers as well as railroad locomotives, needed a lot of tending, were dirty, dangerous, and required frequent maintenance. Diesel engines were an enormous improvement. Caterpillar Tractor Company was already using a diesel engine in their traction equipment, and several manufacturers offered a power plant that was suitable for Case tractors.

The enormous acceptance and wide use of diesel engines for railroad locomotives resulted in increased taxation of diesel fuel. The cash strapped federal government was looking for ways to increase revenues during the Depression and added a tax on diesel fuel in 1934. Locomotives were big users of diesel, and the tax provided a lot of federal revenue. But the increased

price of diesel fuel then made any cost savings for farmers negligible. Case experimented with diesel engines, buying a diesel power plant designed by the Hasselman Company of Stockholm, Sweden, to fit into a modified Case Model L. Sales were slow because supplies were slow, due in great part to some patent litigation against Hasselman. In five years only about 120 Hasselman diesel units had been sold.

But tractors were already running on gasoline or kerosene, both plentiful and reasonably cheap. Gasoline-powered engines were reliable and easy to repair with power to spare. And corporate Case was putting their designers to work on a wide range of powered implements: loaders, balers, choppers, planters—dozens of machines. Case learned a lesson and waited until 1944 to open serious discussions with diesel designer Hans Fischer. So although the Case engineering development group experimented with diesel tractors, it would be nearly twenty years, August of 1953, before the Case diesel powerhouse Model 500 made its debut.

The Flambeaus 1939–1955

At the end of the Depression years and just before the outbreak of war in Europe, dramatic design changes were showing in automobiles, trains, and planes. Many of the changes were made possible by the increased usage of diesel engines and the decreasing reliance on huge, heavy steam boilers. Smaller, cleaner diesel engines gave engineers some new options. Locomotives were being "streamlined" with long, clean lines. And engineers were taking a new look at other equipment as well, including agricultural machinery.

Along with all the other tractor builders, Case became aerodynamic. The boxy little bulldog tractor disappeared forever, replaced by curves and swerves. The color changed from gray to bright red-orange, known as Flambeau Red. And it was an enormously profitable move. The Flambeau would be the best selling tractor line in all of Case history.

Case Goes Aerodynamic

The design of mechanical equipment had made a major leap forward, this time in response to another new industry, airplane manufacture. The sleek "aerodynamic" design of planes had an enormous impact on both industrial and consumer product design. During the 1930s and 1940s, industrial designers had an extraordinary impact on the shape of machinery. Locomotives, autos, trucks, and planes were all reshaped by designers, responding to the new dictum "form follows function." Most wheeled vehicles, even the ones chugging along at 4mph, at least looked as if they could go as fast as an airplane.

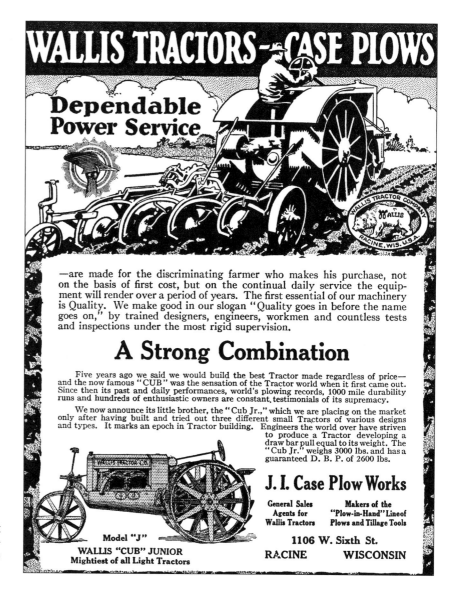

Wallis tractors and Case plows, but note there are no trademark disclaimers in this advertisement from 1917.

The Model L and the Model C were both adapted for use as industrial tractors. The heavy rubber treads made them especially suitable to warehouse use. *J. I. Case Archives*

Four Americans—Henry Dreyfuss, Norman Bel Geddes, Raymond Loewy, and Walter Teague Dorwin, Jr.—are now recognized as the founding fathers of the industrial design profession. They also revolutionized tractor design. John Deere, Henry Ford, and many other manufacturers hired these industrial designers to shape appealing new profiles for their automobiles and their tractors. Responding to the competition, Case also brought in design consultants. And they received some design guidance indirectly, by looking over the new tractor designs commissioned by Deere, Ford, and others. Tractor design was going to take some lessons from sports cars, airplanes, and streamlined trains.

Walter Teague Dorwin, Jr., worked on designs for Ford and Marmon. Raymond Loewy redesigned the Hupmobile in 1930 and then acquired a contract with the Pennsylvania Railroad to "streamline" their steam and diesel locomotives. Norman Bel Geddes also had

an auto manufacturer client, Graham Paige. Henry Dreyfuss worked for Bel Geddes, then established his own firm with such important clients as the New York Central Railroad, Lockheed, and Boeing.

Tractor manufacturers wanted machinery that looked just as appealing to their customers as the auto, train, and airplane industries. Raymond Loewy was the designer hired by International Harvester in the '30s, the designer behind the Farmall shape. Henry Dreyfuss and the Dreyfuss design firm have enjoyed a long and productive relationship with John Deere.

The Depression Baby —the D Series

The arrival of the Model D in late 1939 marked the beginning of another era in Case corporate history. The Model D had an "eagle eye" and a hot paint job. Farmers sat pretty tall in the saddle; implement designers gave the operator a full view of outside gangs of

Case was one of the earliest manufacturers of tractors designed specifically for orchards. Special fenders and high wheel lugs for sandy soils were two orchard tractor accessories. *J. I. Case Archives*

Oversized tires for agricultural tractor applications were developed by B. F. Goodrich in the early '30s after citrus growers started modifying old truck tires to fit steel rims. *J. I. Case Archives*

four-row cultivators or any other implements. The operator could see the field, the controls, and implements all at the same time. The red-orange paint color "Flambeau Red," from the French word meaning *flame*, was named for the Wisconsin region where the famous Case trademark eagle, "Old Abe," had been found.

Once again Case was criticized for lacking innovation in engineering. The chicken roost steering had been retained from their earlier models. Once again they laughed all the way to the bank, secure in their role as the Number Three tractor manufacturer, close behind John Deere and International Harvester. The Model D was a Great Depression baby, conceived during some of the darkest days of the late 1930s. But it came from a company that was doing well in spite of the general economy. Sales trended solidly upwards for Case in the second half of the decade.

The conservative Case corporation had created large cash reserves in the '20s, putting money away for the rainy day. Although Case had to make some sacrifices in the early '30s—cutting salaries, closing a few sales offices, and halting dividends—they still managed to modernize manufacturing plants and expand their

Sandy soils and shallow root systems in Florida citrus groves needed special cultivation implements. A new generation of Case diesel tractors got a new generation of implements. *J. I. Case Archives*

Mechanized sprayers had been used in orchards for decades; now mechanized pruning saws were developed to reduce labor costs. *J. I. Case Archives*

An extremely rare Motor Cultivator, marketed by the Plow Works, only sold for a couple of years. The single front wheel had chain steering. The Plow Works trademark, an upraised plow bottom, substitutes for the directional arrow on the front.

J. R. Gyger of Lebanon, Indiana, is a Case tractor collector. This rare Case 400 orchard tractor is one of his gems.

product line. They brought out only one new model, but Case engineers had put a lot of research and development into it. The standard Model D came with four wheels, a power take-off, and Case's motor lift system, first introduced on the Model CC. This mid-Depression offering was a substantial improvement, not just a repeated version of an earlier design. The Model D was a replacement for the Model C of the previous decade. It was built for the farmer who was pulling two, three, or four plows.

By the end of the Depression, Case had brought out the Model D and the Model DC and had three additional new models on the drawing boards. In addition, they introduced a few new implements—a corn picker-sheller, hammer feed mills, and a small combine. The Model D itself, with all its permutations, sold nearly 390,000 tractors over its fifteen year life span, and it remains a favorite with collectors today. The Model D enjoyed a long life span and matured considerably during its time. By the time the model line was ready to retire in the early 1950s, it had acquired disk brakes, hydraulic lifts, and the "Eagle Hitch."

The D series offered as many models as the earlier C series which came out in the '30s. The C series had demonstrated that offering a range of models designed for different field conditions would pay off. So the D

A beautifully restored Case orchard tractor with Flambeau fenders, owned by J. R. Gyger.

was built in nearly a dozen configurations; the DO orchard tractor, the DV vineyard tractor, the DCS for sugar cane fields, the DI industrial tractor, and one called a DC-3, not an airplane but an early model with a three-speed transmission.

One of the first improvements made to the Model D was a new transmission. The improved D now had four speeds rather than three and under the right conditions could jam along about at 10mph. It was a tractor the kids liked to drive as well as the grownups. And when Dad broke down and bought some of the options, well hey, you could really turn heads. This tractor had curved, aerodynamic fenders and real gauges to go along with the hot paint job. Optional equipment included headlights, a muffler, and a cushioned seat. A cushioned seat on a tractor! Can you beat it?

The Model D started out with a hand clutch and then finally switched to a foot clutch late in the model run. The literature said it had "50 modern conveniences that are easily found" but since most of them were mechanical improvements, they couldn't quickly be spotted unless you were driving. But the fenders, headlamps, and the cushioned seat, well, anybody could see those right away.

The distinctive Flambeau Red paint was a Case trademark, just like Old Abe on the Case sign. J. R. Gyger is the owner of this extra-special orchard tractor.

The V and the VA

The V series was the smallest tractor series in the Flambeau line. Suited for small farmers and truck gardeners, it had about 22hp. The V came in only four flavors, but the replacement VA offered a dozen different configurations. It's curious to think of the VA as a replacement since the two models had no major parts in common. However, it was wartime, parts were in short supply, and manufacturers were scrounging to find suitable materials where they could. Case refers to VA as a "replacement" based strictly on size.

The first Vs were built using components from other manufacturers. The engines were built by Continental Motors, and the transmissions were built by Clark. The V series was offered as a standard model, a row crop, an orchard tractor, or an industrial tractor. It came out in 1939, the same time as the Model D, and the two new tractors were meant to replace their two predecessors, the L and the R. The V was built for less than three years before being replaced by an entirely redesigned VA.

Historian Peter LeTourneau observes that the VA tractor is to the Case collector what the John Deere Model B is to the Deere enthusiast. The replacement VA arrived in 1942, with the usual basic models and all sorts of kinky new configurations, some of them designed to fill wartime requirements as tow equipment. Like the Model D, the shape of the VA also evolved over its fifteen-year life span, and the fully matured VA looks a lot different than the early models. The chicken

Man meets crossmotor—and there was still one a size larger! But the chime whistle just came in one size. From the Boonville, Missouri, steam show, 1994.

Always insist on genuine Old Abe parts. A detail from Dennis Ficken's crossmotor.

roost steering disappeared in 1946, the Case Eagle Hitch and hydraulic lift showed up in 1949, and electric starters became common by the end of its life span.

The Series S

The S Series came out in 1940, positioned between the D Series and the V Series. It was offered in five configurations: the plain vanilla S, a row crop tricycle, a row crop with a standard axle, an orchard model, and an industrial version. It was marketed as a smaller version of the D, with similar styling. But it was a strange offering, because it was so close in size and capability to the V which had come out just a year earlier. Some historians surmise that the S was designed to match the competition's models; Farmall had a similar sized tractor.

They both had the chicken roost steering arm and a goose-neck front wheel support. Both had four-cylinder engines, both had a 66in wheelbase, and they were both about the same height. But the Model D was rated at a short 32hp while the Model S was rated ten horses less, coming in at a short 22hp in the Nebraska Test results.

Like the Model D, it had a long life and features were added during the fifteen years it was in production. By the time it was phased out in 1953, it came with standard PTO, electric lights and starter, and all the rest of the Case goodies. But it was apparently not as popular as the VA, probably due to the similarity in size. Both of them were rated about 22hp. But the VA series sold almost twice as many units as the S, over 147,000 units to about 77,000 for the Model S.

Here's half the ignition system for the Model C. Some Case collectors swear that they can get the engine started with just one turn. But you need a strong shoulder.

Here's the magneto and governor, the other half of the new and improved Model C (and Model L) ignition system—the best system that money could buy in 1929.

Dennis Ficken of Boonville, Missouri, positions his little crossmotor.

An Oldie but Goodie, Still Going Strong—the Model LA

Not one to abandon a good thing, Case retained the Model L Series from the Depression years. Updated in 1940, it too got a face lift. Actually it was more of a nose job, a restyled modern grille and a Flambeau Red paint job. During the war Case modified the engine to accommodate diesel fuels, hopefully making it more flexible for service during the war years.

It was a good, solid, heavy-duty tractor. One source calls it the "Workhorse." Produced for thirteen years, there were more than 40,000 around. When added to the numbers for the earlier version of the L, the numbers and longevity are truly impressive. The L and then LA tractors were outstanding performers in the Case stable for about twenty-five years.

Of the four tractors offered (the LA, D, S, and VA), the LA was still the largest offered for general farm chores. It had over 50hp and could pull four to five bottoms, the biggest machine the average farmer would need. "Acres roll by when you hook a 4 or 5 bottom plow to this heavy duty *Flagship of the Flambeau Red Fleet*" says the marketing brochure. Well golly, it makes you want to run right out and buy one, just so you can feel the "acres roll by..."

Model 300, 400, 500—the Diesel Age

The last of the Flambeaus appeared in the early 1950s. They mark the beginning of another important era for Case and the introduction of still another important series of tractor models. Historian Michael Holmes says the Series 500 was the first major change for Case since the Model L appeared in the '30s. The

A detail of the crossmotor belonging to Dennis Ficken.

102

Radiator detail, Case crossmotor.

Radiator detail, Case Model C.

appearance of the 500, 400, and 300 Series tractors featured innovations, and their appearance is a glorious finale in the Golden Age of Tractors.

The 500 was the largest of the three tractors with a six-cylinder engine. The 400 and 300 had four-cylinder motors. This was the first series of tractors built by Case that were driven by gears. The engineers had finally replaced the chain-drive system developed by David P. Davies way back before 1928. Diesel engines were available, or you could get an engine that ran on gas, kerosene, or LP gas. The bodies were restyled, keeping up with automobile designs, and the paint job changed again.

The Model 500 showed up first. The new numbering scheme replaced the alpha designations in a sequence that defies logic, but then so did the letter designations Case used for decades. And to add further confusion, after the 500, Case brought out the 300, and finally the 400. And they used two different paint schemes. The new tractors were to be painted a light tan called Desert Sand. The Flambeau Red was reserved for trim and wheels. But the early 500 tractors were built when the production line was still painting Flambeau Red, so the later models (around 1956) have the two-toned paint.

But let's look at the positive side. Hooray...at last, Case has a diesel! The Model 500 was the first in the new series, introduced in 1952, and this tractor was available with a diesel engine. (After John Deere brought out a diesel in 1949, everyone had to have one.) Although the engine was new and big, a six-cylinder, the transmission was not. Case sold the Model 500 with power steering and a Flambeau Red paint job, the last of the Case tractors to wear all red. The 500 was in production until 1956.

The Model 300 was just like driving the family auto, just a little slower. It had a simple H gearshift pattern, and it featured a new twelve-speed transmission, twelve forward and three reverse speeds. Of course the fastest speed you could travel in the field was a blazing 9mph, but the Case 300 was an economical and flexible little machine. It came with a choice of four fuels and the patented Eagle Hitch with stabilized depth control.

Finally it all came together in the Model 400, a new motor and a new transmission. This was the first, all-new Case tractor in nearly twenty-five years. It came with a three-point hitch, a new paint job, and a new attitude. The company finally replaced the chain-drive transmission that Davies had introduced in 1928. The management at Case was so excited about the 400 that it had a special debut in 1955 in San Antonio, Texas. The 400 could run on a choice of fuels: gas, diesel, or LP gas. It could pull four plows and came in a number of models for all the usual applications—row crop, orchard, industrial, and high-clearance. New engine, new transmission, new paint, new attitude...who could ask for anything more?

The new Case tractors were well received and initial sales were brisk. Unfortunately, a depressed post-Korean war economy slowed sales as America went into a "recession." The economists were afraid to label it a depression. However, the improvements that Case made to its products, especially the 500 Series, are said to have had a permanent impact at John Deere. The two-cylinder "Poppin Johnny" was finally retired in 1960, pushed off the field by the Last of the Flambeaus.

CHAPTER 4

THE IMPLEMENT LINES—
HORSES TO STEAM TO GASOLINE

Which came first, the tractors or the implements? Well as everyone knows, the cart came before the horse—and then followed behind ever after. It's the implements that determine your horsepower needs. How big a tractor do you buy? How heavy are your implements, and how big a job are you doing? Are you farming level land? Are you plowing prairie or river bottoms? Picking a tractor means that you look at the number of plow bottoms first, then buy a tractor big enough for the job.

Tractors changed farming profoundly. While that sounds like a gross simplification, we should consider some of those changes and what that meant to the implement business. Remember that Case had offered steam-powered traction equipment for hauling multiple plow bottoms for decades. What was so new and wonderful about a smaller gasoline tractor doing the same chore?

Well, few farmers used the big steam tractors. They were horribly expensive and only suitable for large, relatively flat acreage. They made it easier to plow if you had a section or two in South Dakota, but the big steamers still had drawbacks. They required an experienced operator; explosions were not uncommon. It took half a football field to turn them. And even with careful use, sparks from the boiler sometimes set the field on fire. There goes this year's harvest, up in flames—and sometimes the house and the barn too.

Now, for the first time in farm history, the farmer did not have to stop working when the horses were tired. It was possible to plow from sunup to sundown, working as long the farmer could safely see the field. The tractor introduced new stresses on the farmer; a longer work day and a potentially dangerous machine. But a new level of prosperity and economic security

Troy dump wagons, built in Troy, Ohio, were one of the many early products that were carried by Case branch houses. *J. I. Case Archives*

Definition of Horse Power

TO designate the power of a motor, steam engine or gas tractor the term Horse Power is used. Horse power is a unit of power and represents the measure or rate of doing work. One horse power represents the amount of power required in lifting 33,000 pounds one foot in one minute, or the equivalent.

The unit of work is the foot pound, and is the amount of work required to lift one pound through a distance of one foot. Horse power, therefore, is the amount of power required in doing 33,000 foot pounds of work in one minute. This may be accomplished by lifting a weight of one pound through a distance of 33,000 feet in one minute; or, for instance, 165 pounds through a distance of 200 feet in one minute,

Since 200 x 165 = 33,000.

It makes no difference how the power is applied or how the work is accomplished as long as the force, the distance it acts through, and the time can be determined.

In the illustration a horse is shown lifting a weight of 150 pounds. If this weight were lifted 22 feet in one-tenth of a minute or at the rate of 220 feet in one minute, the work performed would be one horse power.

Since 150 x 220 = 33,000.

A work horse is capable of exerting a continuous pull equal to about one-eighth its weight. At most field work the horse is required to maintain a pull of about 160 pounds on the traces, although the pull of an implement or a load always varies. For a short period of time, however, a horse is capable of exerting a pull of much more than this but such over-exertion cannot be maintained without injury to the horse.

The weight and the draft of a load should not be confused. The draft of a load of one ton on a wagon on a hard road may be less than 100 pounds, while in a field a pull of probably 300 pounds would be required to move that same load. It is the actual pull in pounds and the rate at which work is done that determines the horse power required to pull a load or an implement.

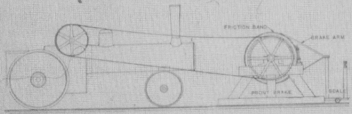

The power of a motor is usually spoken of as the brake horse power, which is determined by a device known as a Prony brake. With this device it is possible to transform the power at the fly wheel into force that may be measured with a scale in pounds. The other factors are also easily found, and the brake horse power of the motor may be readily determined. Such a device is shown in the lower illustration. In all cases a horse power is equal to 33,000 foot pounds in one minute.

Draw Bar Dynamometer

The drawbar horse power of a tractor is found by placing a dynamometer (see illustration) between the tractor and the load pulled. The dynamometer is simply a form of spring scales, suitably proportioned, and is usually provided with a recording device so the pull in pounds is recorded on a card. The rate of travel in feet per minute is then determined. To find the drawbar horse power, the pounds pull is multiplied by the number of feet traveled per minute and divided by 33,000.

If a tractor in plowing exerts an average pull of 2,000 pounds on the drawbar while traveling 2¼ miles per hour, or 196 feet per minute, the drawbar horse power developed will be

2000 x 196 ÷ 33000 = 11.88 horse power.

In rating tractors both the drawbar and motor ratings are usually given, and we speak of 10-20, 12-25 horse power tractors, etc. The power developed by the motor at the fly wheel is, of course, considerably greater than that obtained at the drawbar, because some of the power is used in propelling the tractor itself. The difference does not amount to one-half, however, as indicated by the rating. Case tractors are so designed and constructed that a very high percentage of the motor power is actually delivered at the drawbar.

The rating of Case tractors does not denote the maximum power they will develop. All Case tractors are rated very conservatively, or are really under-rated. This permits a tractor to be used under all conditions, when the draft may vary to a great extent, without having to skimp the work or getting stuck when such conditions are encountered. It also means longer life for the machine and greater satisfaction in its use. There is perhaps nothing so deteriorating and harmful to a machine, and especially to a tractor, as overloading.

FRICTION BAND
BRAKE ARM
PRONY BRAKE
SCALE

Engine Belted to Prony Brake

5

CASE
Hay Tools

1. **Mowers for Clean, Fast Cutting.** Internal Gear Drive. Cutter-bar Alignment a Feature.
2. **Left Hand Rake Saves Leaves and Color.** Inclined Reel. Turn Windrows Without Setting in Wheel.
3. **Drop Deck Loaders.** Large Cylinder Offers Greater Gripping Surface. One or Two Cylinders.
4. **Hay Balers for All Field or Stationary Baling.** Made in Two Sizes—14'x18' and 17'x22'.

J. I. CASE CO. INC.
ESTABLISHED 1842
RACINE-WISCONSIN-U-S-A

An advertisement for Case hay tools which appeared circa 1930. Case had already acquired most of its implement companies by this time and had weeded out the poor performers. *J. I. Case Archives*

Above right
Case was rightfully proud of its association with Grand Detour, the oldest plow builder in America. This design salutes that special partnership. *J. I. Case Archives*

Grand Detour made an entire line of plows from a simple, single-bottom to this complex engine plow designed to be drawn by steam traction. *J. I. Case Archives*

could now be achieved. It was now possible to "beat the weather." Farmers could harvest a crop quickly if a storm was coming, and he could do it alone. The tractor had some other features. You could park a tractor and go away for a week. You couldn't park the horse; it still needed to eat.

A smaller, more affordable tractor brought new flexibility to farming and offered the farmer increased independence and economic security. While we always talk about the difference the tractor made, we overlook the obvious. It wasn't the tractor that made farming easier, it was powering the implements.

Case Offers Implements

Farmers quickly discovered that implements suited for draft animals were not suitable for tractors. The attachment points were different, the drawing stresses were different, and a 12hp machine exerted a lot more force than a three-horse hitch. That new, big-horse-power tractor could pull a cultivator to pieces in just a few days. Modifying old implements worked for a while, but as tractor use became widespread, new and improved implements were being developed.

Case had been in the implement business for a number of years, developing plows for use with their big steam tractors. And they had gotten into related lines such as water wagons and tenders to accompany their steamers. Case offered a selection of tillage equipment through the J. I. Case Plow Works, although plows developed especially for the smaller gasoline tractors were coming from the parent company.

By the time the J. I. Case Threshing Machine Company started selling gasoline tractors in 1912, it had already become a full-line agricultural machinery dealer, primarily through its branch houses. The regional sales networks, branch houses, and sales "travelers" offered local farmers a range of wagons and implements suited to local crops and soil conditions. While

The expression "Power Farming" first came into use around 1910, and the copywriters used the term generously. *J. I. Case Archives*

107

GRAND DETOUR PLOWS

1837

TRADE MARK REG. U.S.A PAT. OFF. AND IN FOREIGN COUNTRIES

BRANCH HOUSES

Where Stocks of Machinery, Repairs and Supplies Are Carried for Quick Delivery

UNITED STATES

ARIZONA—Phoenix.
ARKANSAS—Stuttgart.
CALIFORNIA—San Francisco; Los Angeles.
COLORADO—Denver.
FLORIDA—Tampa.
GEORGIA—Atlanta.
ILLINOIS—Dixon; Peoria; Freeport.
INDIANA—Indianapolis.
IOWA—Des Moines; Mason City; Sioux City; Waterloo.
KANSAS—Wichita.
KENTUCKY—Louisville; Lexington.
LOUISIANA—Crowley.
MASSACHUSETTS—Boston.
MICHIGAN—Lansing.
MINNESOTA—Minneapolis; Mankato; Fergus Falls.
MISSOURI—Kansas City; St. Louis.
MONTANA—Billings; Great Falls; Lewistown; Glasgow.
NEBRASKA—Lincoln; Sidney.
NEW YORK—Syracuse.
NORTH DAKOTA—Fargo; Dickinson; Bismarck; Williston; Minot; Devils Lake; Grand Forks.
OHIO—Columbus.
OKLAHOMA—Oklahoma City; Enid.
OREGON—Portland.
PENNSYLVANIA—Harrisburg.
SOUTH DAKOTA—Sioux City; Watertown; Aberdeen.
TENNESSEE—Nashville.
TEXAS—Amarillo; Dallas.
UTAH—Salt Lake City.
WASHINGTON—Spokane.
WISCONSIN—Madison; Oshkosh.

CANADIAN

ALBERTA—Calgary; Edmonton.
MANITOBA—Winnipeg; Brandon.
ONTARIO—Toronto.
SASKATCHEWAN—Regina; Saskatoon.

EXPORT ORGANIZATION

Branch Houses and Dealers in practically all agricultural countries.

J. I. Case Threshing Machine Company

Incorporated

RACINE :: WISCONSIN :: U.S.A.

Grand Detour plows were sold by the Case Threshing Machine outlets starting around 1915. In 1919, Case finally bought the entire company. *J. I. Case Archives*

Case did not actually manufacture most implements, the branch houses that sold the Case line also sold attachments that fit nicely and were featured in Case advertising.

Sometimes Case worked out a joint advertising arrangement. Case tractors proudly pulled Grand Detour plows. "A Case Tractor and Grand Detour Plow Makes a Real One-Man Outfit" says the brochure in headline type. Changes in the size of the family farm were going to have a big impact on Case business. Case was going to need to sell to that "one-man" outfit.

Waves of immigration to the farms continued after the turn of the century. The American Midwest was now dotted with hundreds of small farm towns, built along the railroads. The Great Plains still offered enormous opportunity as the original homestead lands were now subdivided into smaller farmsteads by the sons and daughters of the pioneers. Even the railroads sold farms. A whole new generation of American dreamers were going to try their luck at farming. They didn't know it yet, but they were going to need an affordable general purpose tractor with an assortment of implements to be successful. Case didn't know it yet either.

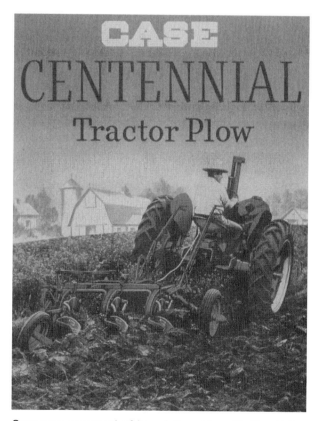

Case was so proud of its relationship with Grand Detour that it marketed a special series of plows as the Centennial plows. *J. I. Case Archives*

Emerson-Brantingham was a company with a long and venerable tradition. Founded in 1860, it was known as the Emerson Talcott Company in 1871. *J. I. Case Archives*

The early tractors were too heavy and too clumsy for general farm work. Even the smaller machines sometimes used for plowing and cultivating had very limited capabilities. They were too big to cultivate row crops, too heavy and slippery to use in a wet field, and too clumsy to turn in close quarters. Farmers were keeping their draft animals, not replacing them with a tractor. So the tractor was an additional expense to the farmer, not the money-saving replacement touted in the farm magazines.

Implement design lagged tractor building. And unfortunately there was no standardization among imple-

ment builders. Every tractor had a different hitch arrangement for attaching implements. Farmers found that if they bought a different brand of tractor, they usually had to buy all new implements, too. Implement dealers were sometimes forced to carry a wide range of options in order to fit dozens of tractors on the market.

But implement design would be changing, profoundly influenced by tractor usage. As tractors also became lighter and more maneuverable, the tractor itself was used more as an implement and less for draft purposes. Farmers who kept their draft horses preferred lighter plows and cultivators designed for their

Emerson-Brantingham was known for its foot-lift plow, a design that was so perfectly balanced that a small man could lift the weight of over 500lb of plow bottoms. *J. I. Case Archives*

animals and frequently used the lighter implement with their new tractors. But the pulling points and lines of pull were still radically different. Horses pull from their chests; tractors pull from the drawbar. One is several feet off the ground, the second is sometimes half as high. Implements needed to be rebuilt in order to work efficiently.

Off in the distance, the old-fashioned horse, as well as the Fordson, the John Deere, and the Farmall, were changing farm operations. Farmers had been accustomed to either using their horses or tractors for pulling. Sometimes they used the tractor as a stationary power unit, belted to a thresher or baler. But the combination of a maneuverable gasoline tractor and an implement would make all sorts of farm chores easy. And in a few years, the power take-off) would be refined and moved to the back of the tractor. Then it would be possible to have a tractor and a motorized implement, both powered from the same little engine. Case would not only have to keep up with the tractor competition, Case would need matching implements to stay even.

Case Gets a New Hand on the Wheel

By the mid-1920s, tractor development competition had taken a new turn altogether. These were prosperous times, money for new manufacturing ventures seemed to be readily available, and farmers were ready to buy new equipment. World War I had created a labor shortage as thousands of young men left the farm to see Paree. And you couldn't keep them on the farm when they returned. Tractors were the answer to a serious labor shortage, and equipment manufacturers were responding to the market.

Meanwhile, the J. I. Case Threshing Machine Company was having a spot of trouble. It was still the world leader in the manufacture of threshing machines but was having to compete with newer and more sophisticated combines manufactured by McCormick. It was phasing out its clunky old steam traction engines in favor of newer, lighter gasoline tractors but was running into stiff competition from Fordson, Farmall, John Deere, and a handful of others. It's management was maintaining the conservative values and midwest-

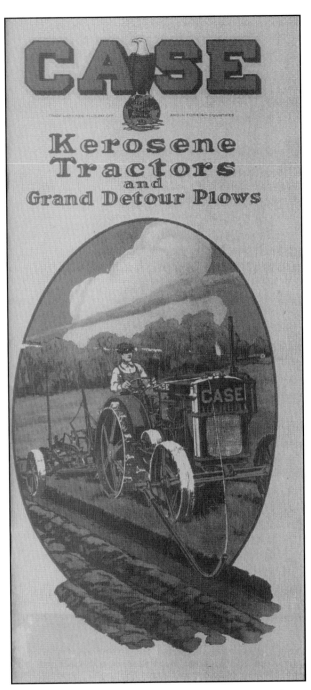

Case advertised Grand Detour plows on their catalogs. Here is a 10-18, rated for pulling two or three bottoms, with a plow specially designed for tractor use. *J. I. Case Archives*

ern work ethic of the Case family, but engineering was falling behind, and profitability was disappearing.

The money managers at Case were concerned and decided that new leadership was needed. The brokerage firm of Morgan, Stanley, Inc., handled stock issues

for J. I. Case Threshing Machine Company, and they had their eye on an executive that could provide some strong leadership in Racine. His name was Leon Clausen, and he was a vice president at John Deere in Moline, Illinois. Clausen was on the board of directors at John Deere, and the head of manufacturing operations. Could he be persuaded to make the change?

Reluctant at first, Leon Clausen finally accepted the position at Case and provided the direction and tenacity that assured the company's survival. When Clausen arrived in 1924, the Case company had been featuring implements in their catalogs for a dozen years. Litigation with the J. I. Case Plow Works kept them from offering Case plows for their tractors, but other plows were available. And the Case branch houses also offered implements. Clausen was going to refine

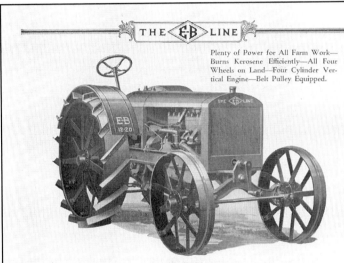

Emerson-Brantingham had a line of tractors, too, but Case preferred to sell their own. *J. I. Case Archives*

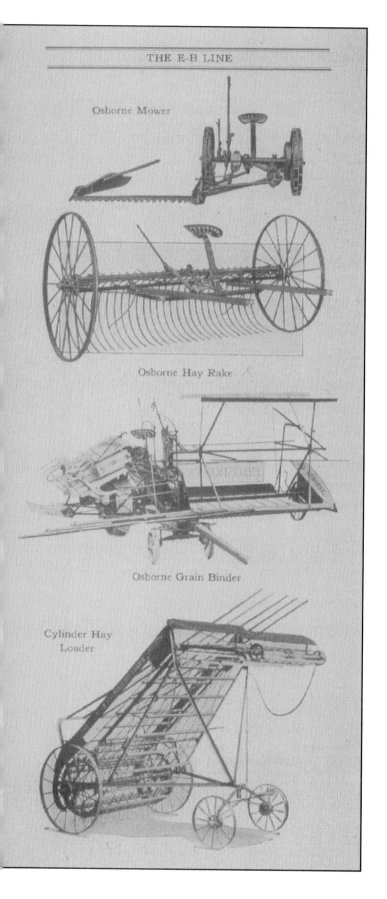

THE E-B LINE

Osborne Mower

Osborne Hay Rake

Osborne Grain Binder

Cylinder Hay Loader

and redesign the implement line. And he would make sure Case had a new tractor to pull them.

An Implement for Every Occasion

Leon Clausen made a couple of extremely critical decisions when he came to Case. He quickly redirected the engineers to design a completely new tractor, an effort which resulted in the Model L and Model C. And he acquired a number of implement companies that could provide suitable accessories for the new tractor.

Clausen can probably be credited with determining which implements would continue to be included in the Case lineup, although he is sometimes criticized, later on, for having been too conservative in implement design. And there is no doubt that he made a very bad decision by delaying the development of a hay baler that used twine instead of wire. But he did acquire several companies with an enormous range of attachments. And since Case did have the first hay baler that picked up hay, maybe we can overlook the twine decision.

The Grand Detour Plow Company—1915

Grand Detour was one of the oldest and finest names in plows and tillage equipment. Like Case, it was another highly respected and venerable American company, known as the only plow maker in America in continuous business since the plow was first developed. The plow company was named for the town where it was located, Grand Detour, Illinois.

Located on the Rock River, the town is situated on a wide ox-bow bend of the river, hence the name, Grand Detour. Founder Leonard Andrus picked the site because the river was a navigable waterway with a good landing site and because it offered a source of hydraulic power. Founded in 1834, his little town prospered as he developed several businesses. He opened a saw mill, a blacksmith shop, and in 1838, he started a stage line. A native of Vermont, Andrus invited another Vermont man to work as a mechanic on the new stage line. John Deere accepted the opportunity and with Andrus developed the first steel plow in 1837.

Deere and Andrus continued to work together for nearly ten years, building a factory which was producing 1,000 plows a year. But around 1847, John Deere moved down river and started his own company in Moline, Illinois. Andrus continued on with new partners and new developments in plow design. Andrus'

The E-B company had acquired the Osborne line, which included the famous Osborne binder and other implements. *J. I. Case Archives*

Corn was always tougher to pick than the other grains.
This horse-drawn picker is operating in the late 1920's.
J. I. Case Archives

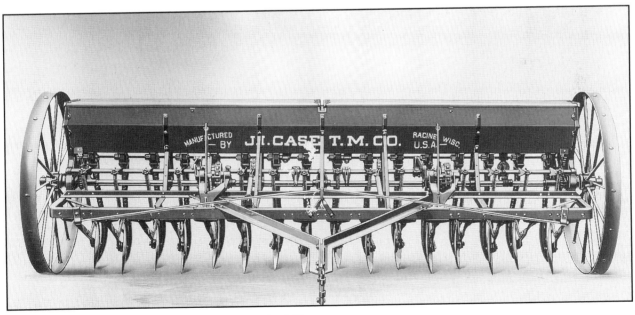

Case built a few implements of their own. This drill
carries the name of the Threshing Machine Company.
J. I. Case Archives

Case sold implements for rice farming. Here are some implements for rice growing and harvesting. *J. I. Case Archives*

name was dropped from the company at his death; the company again became simply The Grand Detour Plow Company. It was an industry leader, expanding its line with cultivators, spike tooth harrows, disc plows, and several models of the extremely popular sulky plow.

The J. I. Case Threshing Machine Company was in a dilemma. They needed to offer farmers a suitable plow for use with their tractor, but the J. I. Case Plow Works was suing them. Under the circumstances, they could not market products from the Case Plow Works equipment line. They tried offering plows from the Sattley Company, and one catalog advertised a Case-Sattley plow. The Sattley Company president, Herbert Miles, was married to Flora Erskine, daughter of Massena Erskine. Massena Erskine had been a founding partner of the J. I. Case Threshing Machine Company, so it seemed that Sattley might be a suitable partnership. But the Wisconsin Supreme Court decision stated that the name Case could appear only on plows manufactured by the J. I. Case Plow Works. The Case-Sattley plow was dropped, and a new supplier had to be found.

The Threshing Machine Company then formed an alliance with the Grand Detour Company, an engagement that became a marriage in 1919 when Case bought Grand Detour. Case continued to use the Grand Detour name on plows and other tillage equipment until 1928 when Clausen reorganized the implement lines. In the meantime, Case continued to use the Grand Detour name and was careful to print a disclaimer:

"NOTICE: We want the public to know that our plows and harrows are Not the Case plows and harrows made by the J. I. Case Plow Works Co."

Oregon horse farmers Bob Oswald and Sarah Fryer wouldn't part with their Case sulky plow. They breed Suffolk punches, a breed of draft horse that really loves to pull, so they keep a small collection of antique implements to amuse their horses.

The Emerson-Brantingham Company—1928

Another highly respected farm implement manufacturer in the Midwest, the Emerson-Brantingham Company (E-B), could trace its lineage back to about 1853. The Dave Erb-Eldon Brumbaugh history of the Case company points out that there were 1,943 agricultural equipment manufacturers in 1880. While many of them disappeared in the national depression of the 1890s, they seem to have been somehow replaced after World War I by hundreds of gasoline tractor and automobile manufacturers.

A crossmotor pulling a combine. Cutting and threshing has now changed from an operation requiring two dozen people to an operation that just needs two. *J. I. Case Archives*

A hay baler, one of the implements developed by Case implement designers. For many years, Case had the only hay baler available on the market. This one is operating just after the start of World War II. *J. I. Case Archives*

An early, horse-driven hay baler. *J. I. Case Archives*

The machine that made Case famous, a combine. This horse-powered version is harvesting in Endicott, Washington, in 1930. *J. I. Case Archives*

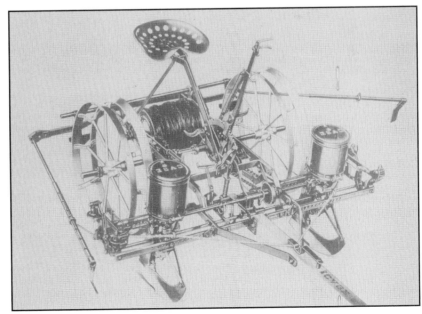

The Case corn planter comes in two versions: horse-drawn or tractor-drawn. But either version lets you plant absolutely even rows of corn with regular spacing, important for easier cultivation and harvesting. *J. I. Case Archives*

Maybe it's the best of both worlds, a Case corn harvester with a pair of Belgians in their finest fly nets.
J. I. Case Archives

It's the front side of a Case seed drill, set up to be pulled by six horses if you've got that many. Planters and drills were part of the implement lines sold by Case distributors, and although the Case name is on the product, most of the implement lines came from other manufacturers. *J. I. Case Archives*

Case was hedging its bets with this corn binder, appealing to both the horse farmer and the farmer with a new Case Model L tractor. *Halberstadt Collection*

Below
The corn binder was an implement that opened an entirely new market to Case. A traditional leader in threshers, Case sales for many years were primarily to wheat farmers. *Halberstadt Collection*

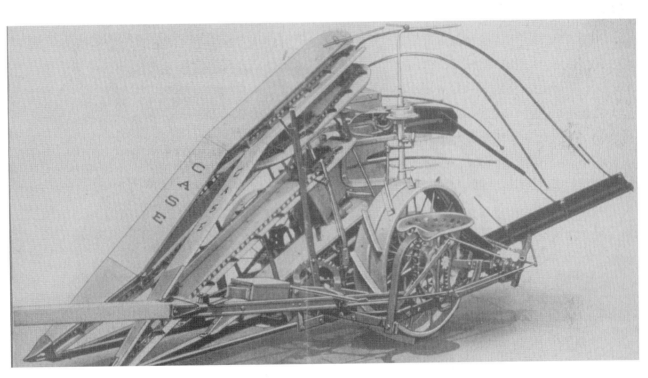

The PTO on the Case tractor allowed this to be a one-man operation—Power Farming in action. This configuration shows how the tractor can simultaneously provide power for the corn binder and the wagon loader while pulling a wagon. *Halberstadt Collection*

Case celebrated the 100th anniversary of the plow with the Centennial Tractor Plow. The anniversary actually belongs to the Grand Detour Company, founded in 1837. It's a little reminder to John Deere & Company that Grand Detour bottoms were a Rock River rival. *J. I. Case Archives*

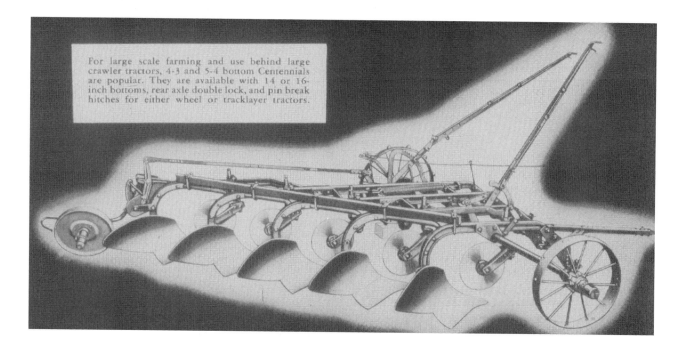

Agricultural equipment was big, big business when most of America lived on the farm. The ag equipment business changed quickly, and there was always some new machine being sold in the marketplace. Competition was overtaking companies that made bad choices, and the venerable Emerson-Brantingham Company was in deep trouble when Case came to the rescue.

A corporation with a wide product line which included tillage equipment and wagons as well as a line of gasoline-powered tractors, Emerson-Brantingham found itself in serious trouble during the twenties. It had expanded quickly before World War I, primarily by buying out a dozen or so small manufacturers.

While some of these smaller companies had solid, well-designed machines and implements, other equipment was shoddy.

The 1920s were years of recession for the farm industry, and Emerson-Brantingham had to close a number of its factories. Like many other dealers, they carried a line of gasoline tractors but had to abandon manufacture altogether by 1926. The E-B Company carried the Reeves, Big Four, and Geiser tractors, and they all disappeared from production in the mid-'20s as the parent company faded. When Case finally acquired the E-B Company, only the agricultural and farm machinery divisions were purchased. Then Case continued to weed out the poorly

EASIEST PLOW TO HANDLE
... to Adjust

Left
Case remembers the field requirements of large scale farmers with a five-bottom plow. Hopefully, the customer owns a Case tractor with some hefty horsepower to pull all those bottoms. *J. I. Case Archives*

The competition had developed and patented a system of draft control; this hydraulic arrangement is one Case solution. *J. I. Case Archives*

The alternative to Case hydraulic control was the Oil-Bath Power Lift. This Case VAC came equipped with hydraulic lift control, but the advertisement details the benefits of the Oil-Bath Power Lift, giving farmers another option. *Halberstadt Collection*

made and unprofitable implements, abandoning duplicate products such as spreader wagons that were already included in the Case catalog.

Case acquired a few valuable assets from the Emerson-Brantingham deal. It received the extraordinary Osborne foot-lift plow, a mechanism so nicely designed that even a child could lift the weight of several plow bottoms. They also acquired a network of E-B dealerships, a manufacturing facility in Rockford, Illinois, and a line of grain binders and hay-making equipment that were not in the Case product line. They also acquired corn drills, planters, and binders, especially the Osborne binder, that were sorely needed in the Case catalog.

The Osborne Grain Binder was recognized as the best in the industry and had been distributed by Emerson-Brantingham starting about 1918. Osborne had been a leader in reapers and binders and was first distributed by International-Harvester Company. However, antitrust actions required I-H to sell Osborne which was purchased by Emerson-Brantingham. Then in 1928, Case acquired the Osborne company as part of the E-B company acquisition.

The PTO, the Lift, and the Three-Point Hitch

There were several important developments in tractor design over the years that changed implement usage. All of these were first developed by other tractor builders, but the entire tractor industry quickly adopted these improvements because they were so useful—and so popular. These engineering milestones included the rear-mounted PTO, which appeared in 1929, and the motorlift, which appeared in 1935. The PTO made it possible to use power from the tractor engine to provide power to an implement while the tractor was being driven up and down the field. Then the implement could be lifted with a motorlift at the end of the row so the tractor could manage a tight turn. One man could now operate both a tractor and implement with safety and efficiency. One more important feature would come along later in 1949, the three-point hitch.

The three-point hitch gets a lot of attention from historians, because it took so long to develop. When it finally appeared, it became the subject of a lengthy lawsuit between designer Henry Ferguson and auto builder Henry Ford. First developed and refined by the gifted Henry Ferguson for Ford, a lawsuit developed when Ferguson was not properly credited or compensated for the device. Ferguson had first developed it around 1920 as the Duplex hitch, a system of struts that allowed a plow to rise up and over an obstruction encountered in the field. Without this flexibility, the plow would ordinarily hang up on a snag and stop the tractor, sometimes forcing the tractor to rear up. The new hitch made plowing much easier and safer.

The plow still needed some sort of depth control device, and Ferguson continued improving and refining his invention, adding a hydraulic system to the tractor. Now farmers could lift and turn the plow at the end of the row, using the tractor motor for power.

The Grand Detour Plow Company boasted a long tradition, and old-timers would recall its early association with John Deere. It seemed like a suitable replacement for the Case Plow Works. *Halberstadt Collection*

Case acquired a line of rakes, mowers, and related equipment when they bought the Emerson-Brantingham line. They quickly weeded out duplicate product lines and put the Case logo on nearly all their implements. This brochure probably dates from the early depression years of the '30s. *Halberstadt Collection*

Below
Compared to the sulky plow, the sulky rake is just as simple and straightforward and just as uncomfortable a ride. *Halberstadt Collection*

Use a Case Heavy Duty Sulk

For Handling Heavy Hay and Stalks

This popular Case Self Dump Rake is designed to handle heavy crops of alfalfa, and also to stand the heavy work of raking corn stalks. In order to stand up under such hard work, heavier material is used than that put into the ordinary rake. The main frame of the Case Rake is made of 3 x 3 in. angle steel with heavy angle steel front brace and supported by ½-inch truss rods which can be easily tightened to prevent sagging. This keeps the wheels in proper position to carry the load and furnishes a foundation that enables the rake to do its work.

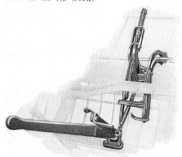

Enclosed Ratchet and Wheel Guard

Handy Lever for Bunching.

Lock Down Device Relieves Operator from Holding Teeth Down.

Extra Heavy 3" x 3" Angle Steel Frame.

Axles Reversible and Interchangeable.

Angle Steel Truss Strengthens Frame.

Strong ½" Spring Steel Teeth.

½" Truss Rod Remains Stationary and Strengthens Frame.

Channel Rim Protects Spokes.

Channel Rimmed Wheels
The wheels of this rake are made in our own plant; they are of the suspension type. Rims are of heavy panel steel which is not

Heavy Teeth
The teeth for this rake are made of ½-inch spring steel with a single coil and round points. For raking alfalfa and corn stalks

A Case sulky rake and a good team put up hay some-time during the early 1930s. This farmer has added a seat cushion. *J. I. Case Archives*

When Ford and Ferguson went to court, other tractor builders quickly developed similar hitches for their machines. Case introduced a similar device which they named the Eagle Hitch in 1949.

While Ferguson was first developing his improved hitch in the 1920s, another talented machinery designer, Edward A. Johnston, was introducing the PTO. First introduced on the McCormick-International Harvester Farmall tractor, this improvement was a direct response to Ford competition. During a visit to France, Johnston had seen a splined extension sticking out the back of a McCormick tractor. He was an experienced engineer, developing improvements for the McCormick thresher and even building a personal automobile.

Johnston recognized that the splined PTO extension operating a binder in France could be modified to operate all sorts of similar equipment. McCormick engineers recognized that a small, all-purpose tractor had to do more than just plow and cultivate. A wide range of powered implements were envisioned; it now became just a matter of development and production. Once introduced, it became widely imitated.

The side-delivery rake made the haying job a little easier, but the seat was still uncomfortable. *J. I. Case Archives*

A toothed harrow breaks up the soil surface in the early spring of 1927. *J. I. Case Archives*

The J. I. Case Threshing Machine Company carried implements built by Emerson-Brantingham. Case would take over more and more of the E-B line and by the end of the decade, all of these implements, including the plows and tractors, would be merged with other Case and Grand Detour tillage equipment. Then Case discarded duplicate product lines, keeping only the best. *J. I. Case Archives*

The Rock Island Plow Company—1937

Case acquired one more full-line implement manufacturer, another pioneer agricultural machinery developer with a line of tractors and implements. Case ignored the tractor lines and acquired only the implements and the manufacturing facilities. The Rock Island Plow Company had been in the Midwest since 1855. By the turn of the century, it had diversified, and their catalog showed seed drills and spreaders, mowers and binders, and stationary engines and wagons. In short, they carried everything a farmer could need—except a tractor. In 1914 they found a tractor firm that would agree to a partnership, the Heider Manufacturing Company in Carroll, Iowa. Two years later Henry Heider sold his tractor company to the Rock Island Plow Company and tractors continued to be built at that plant until Case bought the factory in 1937.

The Case Combine

One of the most common chores for early Case steam traction was hauling combines. A combine is a machine that "combines" two important field operations, harvesting and threshing. One would assume that the world leader in thresher building would also lead in combine development and manufacture. Once again, Case waited until the competition had worked out all the bugs before proceeding with combine construction. Case entered the combine market in 1922, just two years before Leon Clausen took over as president. Clausen improved combine design and proceeded to aggressively develop and produce combines.

Smaller combines were designed as implements. Although they had an individual power unit to cut and thresh grain, they were pulled through the field by a tractor. Large combines were single purpose machines, designed to harvest a single crop. Case began developing combines in the early 1920s, using the same engines that were being used on the crossmotor tractors.

Once again it was the need for a machine which used less manpower that pushed development. Early threshers pulled by horses required teams of men to drive and care for the horses, a threshing crew to operate the machine itself, and a few people to fill sacks with grain and haul the grain to a barn. The development of the combine reduced the manpower from a dozen to just one or two people.

In the '50s, Case was just recovering from the shortages of World War II and was finally producing a significant range of implements. In 1953, Case introduced dozens of new products for use with the new diesel tractors. The new implements included disc plows, lister drills, cotton strippers, and disc harrows.

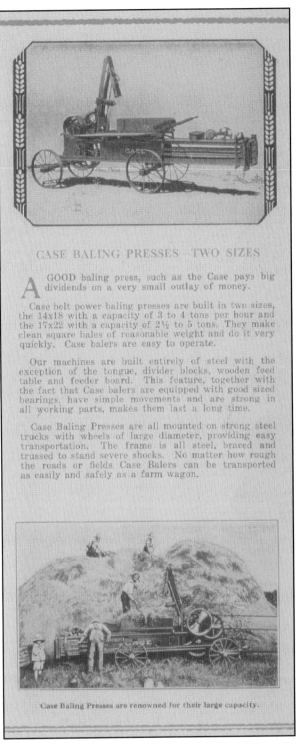

The J. I. Case Threshing Machine Company offered a few important farm implements that other companies rushed to copy. One was the baling press. In a pamphlet from the '20s, a Mr. Livingstone Moffat of Cape Province in the Union of South Africa offers a testimonial, "I would not be without the press and I can recommend it to all farmers needing a press for home work." *J. I. Case Archives*

Sowing wheat, rye, or oats yielded best results when planted with a drill designed just for small grains. A drill allowed uniform planting depth and uniform seed coverage, two critical factors needed in production. *J. I. Case Archives*

The marketing department at J. I. Case was an industry leader in identifying special cultivation needs of various crops. Here they are offering a line of implements specifically for the beet and bean farm, usually a small operation. The RC tractor and implements are set up to be handled by a single operator. *J. I. Case Archives*

Hard times during the Depression kept a lot of small farmers from buying a tractor. This farmer plants corn using a team and corn planter. The extensions allow him to keep all his rows straight for easier cultivation and harvesting. *J. I. Case Archives*

Case liked to point out that their tractors could do several jobs at once. Here a Case Model C is pulling two implements; plowing with double bottoms and then breaking up the soil with a toothed harrow. *J. I. Case Archives*

Case acquired a line of dump wagons from the Troy wagon builders, another line was included in the Emerson-Brantingham purchase, and still another line from the J. I. Case Plow Works buy-out. But by the early 1930s, all the wagons were being trademarked by Old Abe no matter where they were originally designed. *J. I. Case Archives*

A sulky rake and pair rakes clover hay on the Leo Strausburger farm near Lafayette, Indiana, in 1936. *J. I. Case Archive*

A side-delivery rake readies hay for stacking. It was also the implement of choice for raking peas. *J. I. Case Archives*

Junior takes the new tractor for a spin around the south forty. Buying a new Case tractor was advertised as a good way to keep the kids on the farm. *J. I. Case Archives*

Cow peas, field peas, and crowders—lima and soy beans. Most peas, beans, and vetches could be cultivated, mowed, and raked using regular mowers and side-delivery rakes. But to load peas gently, without splitting the pods, a pea loader was the desired implement. *J. I. Case Archives*

Corn binders were first attached to a corn harvester around 1895. This Case binder is cutting and binding ripe corn and then laying the bundles in the field about 1930. *J. I. Case Archives*

Mules were the preferred draft animals in the South, in Texas, and in many farms of the lower Midwest, especially for cotton cultivation. Double furrows are being plowed with this double disc plow. *J. I. Case Archives*

Horse-drawn ridge buster at work, shaping a single ridge. Cotton, beets, and potatoes grow best in ridged furrows. *J. I. Case Archives*

The next year Case brought out twenty-two more new products, including the "disposable" plow. Since blacksmiths had nearly disappeared by the 1950s, sharpening a plow bottom was not always an option. A throwaway plowshare, easily replaced, allowed farmers to keep on going and going and going.

The Series 300, 400, and 500 tractors introduced in the 1950s had a large range of suitable implements, all designed to make farming safe and efficient. But diesel tractors would now begin to dominate; the age of the gasoline tractor would fade. The Case corporation would be concentrating their development in other directions, branching out into construction and industrial equipment. They would still build and develop large agricultural equipment such as combines and harvesters. But the next giant leap forward for Case tractors would take nearly twenty years, when the new CDC diesel engine and a Roll-Over Protection System (ROPS) would reshape the industry.

Dennis Ficken and his Boonville Bonanza

Dennis Ficken is a relatively new tractor collector. He's only been really active since 1983, but his collection of vintage machines is now over eighty vehicles, about half of them Cases. He blames his interest in collecting farm equipment on his father and his friends. Dennis went to work for Firestone after he left college, eventually starting his own tire dealership. But his farm heritage took over, and the collecting really started seriously when some of his customers asked him to join the local steam engine association in Boonville, Missouri.

Dennis grew up on a farm in northern Iowa, and the family's first tractor was an IH-Farmall. Then they moved to southern Missouri, so dad had to sell the first tractor but then bought another, smaller Farmall. He got interested in collecting, starting out with McCormick-Deering, John Deere, and of course, Farmall.

The first Case he bought was out in Fort Leavenworth, Kansas, sitting in a field. "It looked kind of rough and stuck," Dennis remembers. "It was rusted up. It was a *Kansas* tractor. They're not severely rusted up, but they're faded out. It had a flat tire, and they had parked it in a hole. I bought it for $155."

Dennis brought it home and cleaned it up. Then a little later he bought a CC. He acquired the CC because he was interested in participating in pulling competitions, and he reports that the CC pulls real well. But it ruined his reputation. Buying two Case tractors like that, he said, made everybody think he was a "Case man."

A lot of local tractor collectors didn't like the styling of the Case, so when they'd buy one they'd trade it to Dennis for something else in his collection. His reputation as a "Case man" has built his collection. He now has approximately forty different models of Case tractors. "They're easy to work on. They're an old tractor, but no matter how long you have them you can still find parts for them," he reports.

The first Case tractor Dennis fixed up was a 1939 Model Case. Last week his neighbor came by and said, "I've got something you'd really like." He came dragging into the shop with a tool box, and it had the serial number for the 1939 Case on it. He apologetically said, "I took the tool box off that old Case and put it on the side of my dad's Ferguson because it didn't have a tool box that was handy to get to. Now I'm selling the Ferguson, and I know those people won't want a Case toolbox on it." So now Dennis has a highly desirable accessory, made just for his tractor.

Dennis says he likes the Case tractors because of the styling; he really likes that Flambeau Red. He says that he feels the styling is a little more unique than some of the other tractors in his collection. The styling sets Case tractors apart because Case did not try to make every model look the same. So now when anybody around Boonville finds a Case tractor, the first person they call is Dennis. He has also acquired a large supply of "parts tractors," too. And with all of the spares, he can help out other enthusiasts who need parts.

Dennis is frequently asked what his wife thinks about all of this. Dennis responds by cutting straight to the bottom line. First he admits that he has made a little money on tractor swapping. And then he says that his wife always knows right where he is—out in the shop with the tractors.

CHAPTER 5

MAINTAINING THE EDGE—
CASE ENGINEERING

Ask any Case enthusiast why so many Case tractors are still up and running. He'll probably tell you that Case tractors are "over-engineered." What in tarnation is "over-engineering?"

Case can't possibly be "over-engineered;" there have only been two long-term engineering directors on deck since the turn of the century! It seems amazing, but Case engineering for nearly a century has been directed by just two men: David P. Davies and Eldon Brumbaugh. Davies had the first watch, with a career

that finally ended in 1948. Eldon came on board at Case in 1953 and finally retired in 1988. His career covered most of the second half of the century. He has a unique view of Case engineering history since he was both a participant and an observer with a view from the top.

If you ask Eldon Brumbaugh about the Case reputation for "over-engineering," he'll probably tell you that it just means Case tries to do things right. It sounds a lot like what old J. I. Case said to the reporter

Still dripping, tractor parts will be sent to the assembly line when they are finally dry. *J. I. Case Archives*

Here's a rare model, a Case tractor cultivator, probably designed by David P. Davies around 1922. It had a few problems, and it was just not as heavy and solid as the rest of the Case line-up, so additional work was dropped in favor of the crossmotors. *J. I. Case Archives*

David Davies built the engine for his cultivator, a rather tidy little power unit. *J. I. Case Archives*

at the 1876 Philadelphia Exhibition. Case said he built what was "correct in principle and was needed." A good example of "over-engineering" can probably be illustrated by remembering a relatively recent (1969) Case design development, ROPS (Roll-Over Protection Systems). The Case engineers decided to build what was correct in principle and was needed.

Tractors were always dangerous, right from the very beginning. Early tractors were top heavy and frequently rolled over, crushing the driver. Driving on soft soils, hitting a snag, putting a wheel in an unseen hole, or driving on an embankment—those are all routine tractor operations that could turn a tractor over and throw the driver. And don't ask a farmer to strap a safety belt across his lap. It wouldn't have saved many lives in a tractor rollover.

Eldon Brumbaugh had the opportunity to redesign the tractor and the cab. He recalls that in the 1970s the federal government was thinking of mandating safety

"Power Farming" was becoming a new slogan, and Case equipment was making it possible for women to do more of the heavy chores. This 1916 picture of a

Case 9-18 plowing was widely reproduced and was printed in the *Ladies Home Journal* the following year. *J. I. Case Archives*

It was the best of both worlds. That looks like a shiny new Case Model L mowing in the background while the horses are raking and wind-rowing. *J. I. Case Archives*

requirements. The Department of Transportation was thinking about setting some safety standards, and they came around to the Case test grounds, making a survey. They were surprised and commented that Case had a very high safety rating for their equipment, much higher than anyone else in the industry. They asked how Case accounted for the high safety ratings.

Brumbaugh said, "It's simple. When we designed our cab, we designed it for the comfort and convenience of the operator. But Case made a conscious decision. We were only going to make one new cab, and we were going to make it with ROPS. When anyone bought a Case cab, they automatically got ROPS." Safety was not optional.

Now if Case had made two cabs, one with ROPS and one without, and then charged extra for the added safety, they would not have sold any ROPS. It was a design decision that had to be made by the engineers because farmers just wouldn't buy "safety." It had to be

Case Model L provided great power for its size and weight and proved to be a wonderful tool. Here the L is operating a 10ft Power Binder at the Baer farm, northwest of Rockford, Wisconsin. *J. I. Case Archives*

It's hard to believe that Case was not the pioneer in building combines, but J. I. Case Company was a leader in introducing combines to the Midwest and Pacific Coast farms. This Model W Hillside combine is harvesting in hilly Colton, Washington, about 1929. *J. I. Case Archives*

designed into the product. Case knows that farming can be an extremely hazardous job. So Case was the first to make their own roll-over cab.

Building Product Loyalty, One Tractor at a Time

Case built product loyalty, based on their engineering. Eldon Brumbaugh says that it all started with the Case thresher and steam engine. Case took enormous efforts with their steam engines and had an incredible reputation for reliability, decades before they started to build gasoline tractors. Case put the same effort into the gasoline tractors that they put into their steam equipment.

The tractors Case built were very good. The Model L came along in 1929 and was a revolutionary machine. It was really well received. It was built for plowing and open fields. It wasn't a row crop tractor, but it had a very good reputation for reliability. Then Case produced the D and C models. They were a little smaller, built for row crops but were also very reliable.

It was important, however, to maintain an engineering edge over the competition. Case was building tractors before John Deere bought into the market by acquiring Waterloo Boy. And then Deere decided to stick with the little two-lunger rather than going to a four-cylinder engine. Brumbaugh feels that choosing to continue the two-cylinder tractor was an engineering decision by John Deere that actually helped Case sales.

Staying ahead of John Deere and all the rest of them wasn't easy. Case never spent the amount of money, dollar-wise or percentage-wise, for tractor design that Deere did. So from an engineering standpoint, Case had to concentrate on the major things and then use their best judgment on the minor things. Case just didn't have the money to build many prototypes or run thousands of hours. They were always struggling to keep up with the other tractor competition.

Engineering Secrets—Teamwork and an Open Mind

As the former head of Engineering at Case, Eldon Brumbaugh has some observations about technological innovation. He notes that a tractor isn't created by one engineer; it takes a whole group and each engineer contributes. Other companies may work differently. At Allis-Chalmers, for instance, all the patents were issued under the name of their chief engineer, Walter Strales. Everybody in the industry knew that Walter wasn't doing all that work, but he got the recognition. Case has always had a whole group of engineers, each contributing something important to the project, and each one was recognized for his work.

But not even engineering gets all the credit. Case

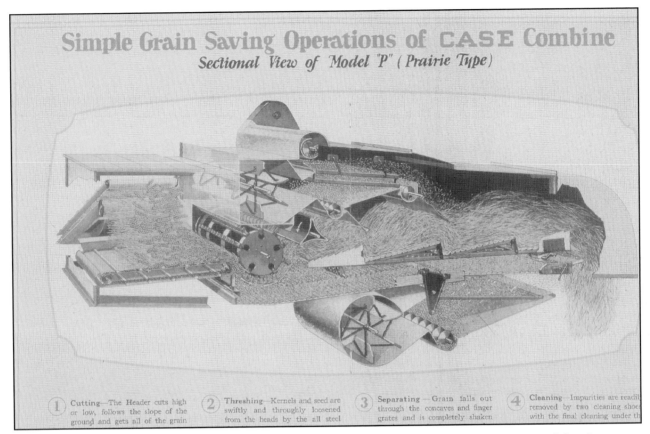

Model P for "Prairie" helped revolutionize harvesting in the west. It was now possible for two or three men to manage an entire harvest that used to be reaped by a threshing crew of a dozen men and scores of horses.

Binders, headers, bundle wagons, and threshers were not necessary when a combine was used. *J. I. Case Archives*

has a saying, "There comes a time when you just have to shoot the engineer and put out your tractor production. If you leave it with the engineer, he'll just keep designing and designing." How do you maintain a technological edge without being the first tractor in the field with the new idea? By letting someone else work out the bugs and not being too proud to recognize a good idea, even if it's not yours.

The gasoline engine was around for many years, but there were a couple of serious problems with the early engines. They didn't have a good spark or good carburetion. Those improvements were evolutionary, and with each one, gasoline engines became better. One engineer concentrates on making a better spark plug or a better magneto, and then it changes the entire industry.

Case has always been willing to try new ideas. When Case engineers first put a torque converter in a tractor, it was not that innovative. There were torque converters on other machines first, but the engineers decided they could take advantage of that technology.

And look at hydraulic systems. Several builders made good hydraulic pumps, so Case bought them. Case used them and improved the performance of their own equipment. When Case first put power steering on tractors, they bought power steering from General Motors. Ideas have to start with someone in the technical area. Marketing people are sales people.

Marketing Versus Engineering

Although customer needs are important to the marketing and sales groups at Case, new tractors and other products originate with Engineering. Most of the innovations in tractor design have come from the technical field—Engineering comes up with the ideas. Marketing organizations can tell the company what the competition already has and how it's selling. Marketing knows what goes on after a product is in the marketplace, and marketing people always try to match the competition. For instance, if John Deere has a new 200hp tractor selling well, and Case doesn't have one, then market analysis will show that Case needs

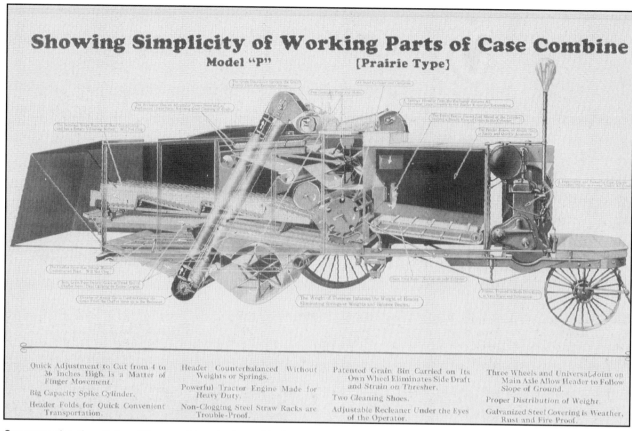

Showing Simplicity of Working Parts of Case Combine
Model "P"   [Prairie Type]

Quick Adjustment to Cut from 4 to 36 inches High Is a Matter of Finger Movement.	Header Counterbalanced Without Weights or Springs.	Patented Grain Bin Carried on Its Own Wheel Eliminates Side Draft and Strain on Thresher.	Three Wheels and Universal Joint on Main Axle Allow Header to Follow Slope of Ground.
Big Capacity Spike Cylinder.	Powerful Tractor Engine Made for Heavy Duty.	Two Cleaning Shoes.	Proper Distribution of Weight.
Header Folds for Quick Convenient Transportation.	Non-Clogging Steel Straw Racks are Trouble-Proof.	Adjustable Recleaner Under the Eyes of the Operator.	Galvanized Steel Covering is Weather, Rust and Fire Proof.

Compare the simplicity of the combine design with the earlier threshers. This machine made farmers independent—no more lost crops because the threshing crews were busy elsewhere. *J. I. Case Archives*

For the more conservative farmer, the Model P combine was still available as horse-drawn equipment. *J. I. Case Archives*

Case combines featured longer and longer header blades. This one is 16ft, but it looks like it can clean the entire field in just two passes. *J. I. Case Archives*

Case continued to sell a full line of implements. The advertising brochure tells you that after harvest season, the Case Tractor Engine can be used as a stationary power unit the rest of the year. *J. I. Case Archives*

The CASE Combine

The Most Substantial Foundation on the Combine for an Engine

The even distribution of the grain, together with the use of two recleaner sieves and a fan blast, in addition to the good work done by the lower shoe, results in exceptionally clean grain.

Case combines deliver cleaned grain that, with well-filled kernels, will test out a strong 60 pound bushel and frequently will sell at a premium.

Plenty of Power

Ample power to drive both the heading and threshing mechanisms is supplied by a heavy duty, four cylinder Case tractor engine. This is the same engine that has given such remarkable success in thousands of Case tractors all over the world. The rated brake horse power at normal speed is 20. The maximum brake power is 25. The normal engine speed is 1050 R.P.M. The cylinders are cast vertically en bloc of special cylinder iron and have a bore of 4⅛ inches and a stroke of 5 inches.

The engine is well lubricated by means of a pressure feed from a gear type oil pump through the drilled crankshaft to the main, connecting rod and cam shaft bearings and to the governor parts. A pressure valve controls the oil pressure and a gauge shows the amount. The crankcase reservoir is equipped with oil level petcocks.

An enclosed, centrifugal-ball type, throttling governor keeps just the correct speed, no matter what the work or load is. The cylinder head is easily removable for cleaning out the carbon or grinding the valves. Renewable cylinder barrels are an important advantage of this engine.

The motor is mounted crosswise on the main frame to secure (1) the most effective and durable drive, and (2) the most substantial foundation about a combine for an engine. A multiple, dry disk type clutch is used. It is fully enclosed, and is built as a part of the engine. A unit control

and at the same time accelerates the motor. When the clutch is again disengaged, the motor is automatically throttled to a low speed.

Simple and Durable Drive

The drive from the clutch pulley to the cylinder is by an endless rubber belt with an adjustable tightener. Both pulleys are lagged, one pulley has two flanges and the other one flange. This belt drive is the highest type and best grade of rubber and has proven to be the most satisfactory, the most durable and the most economical type of main drive. It requires much less attention than other forms of main drives. A steel roller chain drives the separating mechanism from the cylinder while all other drives are by steel link chains.

Engine can be Removed

The engine, which is mounted in a frame of channel steel, can be readily removed from the combine when not in use in the field. It can be mounted on a truck or any other suitable foundation and used as a stationary or portable source of power. This handy power unit furnishes excellent power for silo filling, corn shredding, feed grinding or any of the many farm belt-power requirements.

Built to Last a Long Time

Following this examination of the various parts which make up the combine, a study of the machine as a whole will show you why Case combines are so unusually dependable and durable as well as savers of time, labor, grain and money. The sturdy construction and careful workman-

The Powerful Case Tractor Engine can be Easily

A two-man threshing operation, the Case Model L and a new all-steel, 9ft combine. This combination put a lot of horses out of business. *J. I. Case Archives*

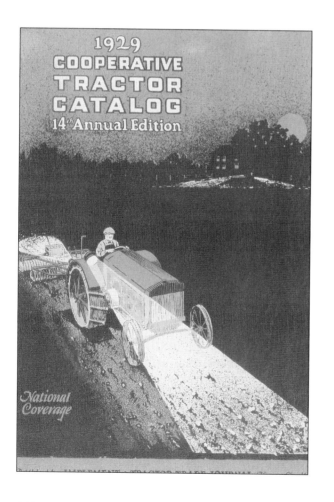

Tractor and implement builders were really competitive. This independent catalog rates the builders and lists 40 tractor manufacturers. Farmers once worked from dawn to dusk; this catalog shows them plowing at night too. *J. I. Case Archives*

one. But by then it is frequently too late to develop a new 200hp machine—you could never catch up.

That doesn't mean that Engineering can ignore the consultants and that the Case company refuses to listen to marketplace reality. In 1923, Case knew that the agricultural equipment market was changing. They hired a special consultant, G. B. Gunlogson, to give them a detailed report. His findings were not really surprising. He noted there was a tremendous need for a small, relatively inexpensive tractor that would serve the farmer with less than 160 acres. And in addition, Gunlogson recommended that Case abandon their motor car industry. (The Case Company manufactured autos and even airplanes at one time.) So Case began to focus on expanding the gasoline tractor lines. They also acquired several implement businesses for their new tractors.

But years later Case still had a reputation for ignoring the "wish lists" of customers and the marketing groups. Eldon Brumbaugh related this story from Hank Hudson about Case corporation president Leon

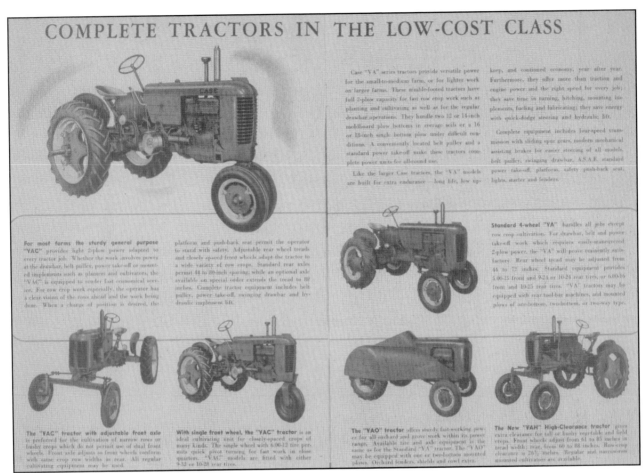

COMPLETE TRACTORS IN THE LOW-COST CLASS

The V Series tractors with the Flambeau Red paint became Case's best-selling tractor line. It was set to compete with the smaller Ford and John Deere tractors, and with the hot paint job, it outdistanced and outclassed the competition. And you could find it in a cornfield. *J. I. Case Archives*

R. Clausen. It neatly illustrates part of the company's attitude about market analysis.

Hank Hudson, one of the plant managers from the Rock Island facility, was visiting president L. R. Clausen in his office in Racine. Sales manager Bill Clark walked in with a new salesman. Hank tried to leave, but Clausen waved him back to his seat. "Sit down, this will just take a minute."

The new salesman was introduced and started immediately talking about the tractors. "What we need is this, this, and this," he began, listing features that he hoped would be on future models. Clausen turned around to his old rolltop desk and opened a copy of the sales catalog. "You were hired to sell what's in this book. You can't sell it, then you don't belong here."

Balancing the requests from marketing with a new, well-engineered product is always a careful judgment call. Product improvements don't always increase sales. A 1946 survey showed that farmers wanted more features

on their equipment. They wanted a foot-operated clutch (like their automobiles), a cab, replaceable oil filters, and a diesel engine. But would these new features sell more tractors, or would buyers shy away from "frills?"

Case engineers know that in order to be successful, you have to design a tractor which is going to meet the needs of 80 to 90 percent of the agricultural market. There are always a few farmers who are going to want something extra, who will try to "hot rod" their equipment. At one time, there was a proposal for building an engine with a torque-topper to run LP gas with diesel. It just wasn't feasible to try and sell a tractor to the general farmer that has to run on two kinds of fuel. While everyone knows that some farmers retrofit their tractors as a torque-topper, you can't sell one in the general marketplace. The needs of the majority have to be met first.

It's difficult to predict the sales potential of new products. Will all the farmers go for a torque-topper or a new transmission, or just a few? When Case market-

Introduced around 1940 just as World War II was starting, the versatile V Series came with enough options and attachments to keep the smallest farmers productive during the labor shortage. *J. I. Case Archives*

The Model D came into production at the beginning of World War II, retaining the chicken roost arm but equipped with bolt-on fenders and deeply dished wheels. Later models were equipped with the Eagle Hitch, and the brochures advertised "eagle-eyed vision" and "quick-dodge steering." This is one of the earlier, clunkier models, plowing along in 1939. *J. I. Case Archives*

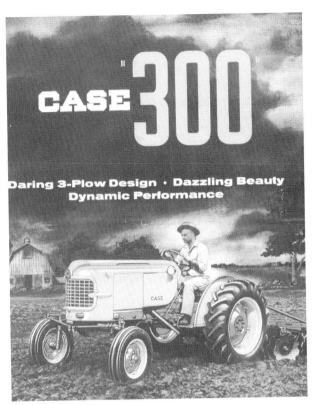

Daring, dazzling, dynamic, diesel! Finally, Case gets a diesel engine, although the Case 300 is available with a gasoline engine too. The sales propaganda says the new 300 is refreshingly new with dazzling beauty. Well, it must be in the eye of the beholder, although it is a right nice machine. *J. I. Case Archives*

ing reports that John Deere has a powershift transmission that is selling well and then says Case should build one, they can usually present good information. But what happens when Case develops the powershift transmission and then asks marketing to evaluate potential sales of a new item? Predicting market acceptance is nearly impossible.

Eldon Brumbaugh has an observation about the difficulty that engineering can get into when they listen to the marketing department.

"When Case came out with the Model 500 diesel, it was partly because farmers were making engine conversions in the field. People were modifying the LA tractor, keeping the transmissions and attaching Caterpillar engines or GM engines. So the marketing department at Case said, 'We gotta have a diesel.' But they looked at what was happening in the field and suggested that the new diesel be modified to take care of all of the old tractors too."

"So the engineers designed the rear of the new diesel engine with a flange that would fit the old LA

transmission. And they also made the engine so it could be adapted to fit the new Model 400 tractor. That flange cost another $1.50 per engine on every engine that Case built. How many conversions were actually made—none. Why? If you think about it, the answer is simple. Why would a farmer spend that kind of money to fix up an old tractor with a new engine, when he can buy a brand new tractor for about the same cost?"

Solid Engineering Builds Solid Success

Some folks say that one of the secrets of Case's success is that they did not make too many changes all at once. The first tractors looked just like the steam tractors. Then the early crossmotors arrived with a few additional improvements, but the chassis and drive mechanism were similar to designs developed for the early steamers.

When you look at the driving mechanism of the early steam engines, you see that the steam had to cross the drive shaft to drive the wheels. The gearing was all in one straight line. So when the crossmotor engine was developed, the easiest way to connect the drive mechanism was to set the motor sideways and connect it through that same shaft. By fitting it sideways, the tractor could still use the older transmission. Fitting it sideways eliminated the need for beveled gears. Case could then concentrate on improving design and performance for later models.

Another secret of solid success was using solid components. From the earliest days of thresher building, Case used parts and assemblies from outside manufacturers and suppliers. As Case built a wider range of products, consistent quality became a greater issue. Case established a testing lab before the turn of the century to test the consistent quality of materials and components. At that time there were still no government standards for materials, so testing was important to ensure consistent quality.

By 1904, Case had built a full laboratory that could measure tensile strength, breaking strength, shrinkage, hardness, and other critical measures of materials. Supervised by a chemist, the laboratory provided an extra measure of product reliability. And, of course, Case mentioned the lab in their advertising.

While Case engineers designed and built a few implements, they concentrated their primary engineering efforts on engines and transmissions. Eldon Brumbaugh observes that implements are easy to make. Just get a piece of steel and bend it. Take it to the field and run it through the ground. If it breaks, get a little heavier piece of steel. The process for building most implements is heat, beat, and bend. When it breaks,

Top Engineer, Eldon Brumbaugh

Good, consistent Case engineering management was responsible for good consistent solid products. While the Case company has experienced a number of changes at the helm over the years, the engineering departments have held steady with consistent guidance. Just two engineering directors managed to span more than a century of Case engineering design. David P. Davies had a lifelong career at Case, starting as a machine shop apprentice in 1886 and finally ending at his death in 1948. He was considered by many to be the Dean of Tractor Engineers in this century.

Standing beside Davies is Eldon Brumbaugh, the engineering director who directed Case design and development for the second half of this century. Starting as a field engineer in 1953, Brumbaugh worked in engineering for thirty-five years. In January 1957, he became head of the tractor works in Racine, eventually consolidating all of the tractor building throughout the corporation to Racine.

The design and development of engines and transmissions, the vital organs of power equipment, came under Eldon's supervision. Any Case equipment lines using engines and transmissions, from tractors to forklifts, from road graders to wheel-loaders, were designed and tested by the development engineers at Racine. In 1972, he became director of corporate engineering, responsible for acquiring many of the other equipment companies such as Poclain and David Brown that were included in the Case family.

Eldon's agricultural machinery career started about the same time as the Age of Diesel. He saw firsthand, and then directed, such developments as ROPS (Rollover Protection Systems) for farmers, a four-wheel-drive tractor, and the development of a brand new, designed-from-scratch, diesel engine for Case equipment. Since he retired in 1988, Eldon participates by writing books on Case engineering history and commenting on agricultural equipment design.

An Indiana native, Eldon was raised in Arizona and went to Arizona schools all his life. When asked about the adjustment between the Arizona and Wisconsin winters, Eldon observed that the Army helped to prepare him during World War II. Observing that his home state was Arizona, the Army thoughtfully assigned him to a ski group during the war. So Eldon had a little experience with snow before he moved to the great white north.

After military service, he returned to Arizona, finishing a degree in mechanical engineering. He was hired by Case in 1953 to work at the proving grounds in Phoenix, Arizona. He said that when he started working for Case, the biggest engine the company had was 60hp. When he left, the biggest engine Case used was 300hp. There was a lot of design development and testing between the two! Mr. Brumbaugh was also an extremely important participant in the research and production of two books on Case: *Full Steam Ahead: J. I. Case, Tractors and Equipment 1842–1955*, co-authored with Dave Erb, and the Case corporate history, *J. I. Case, The First 150 Years*. He is currently working on the second volume of *Full Steam Ahead* with Dave Erb.

---

you can weld a patch on it. Engines and transmissions, however, cannot be patched.

Eldon Brumbaugh Gets a Clean Sheet—Consolidated Diesel

Most engineers never get the opportunity to design a new machine from the ground up. They never get to start with a completely clean sheet of paper. Usually the engineer designs just one part, a new transmission, or a body, but it has to fit with the rest of the existing machine.

Sometimes engineers manage to develop more of a new piece of equipment but still have to keep the old factory, the old tooling, and the old production facilities. The engineer hardly ever gets a chance to sit down with a big white piece of paper and design everything.

Eldon Brumbaugh got that chance—once.

Case needed a new diesel engine, and they had a serious problem. The old engine design had already expanded from 377ci up to 504, from 80hp to about 254hp. The diesel had first been introduced in 1953 and had been used for more than twenty-five years. It was stretched about as far as the rubber would stretch. The diesel was as large as it could go with the existing design. In addition, all the tooling and manufacturing facilities used to build the diesels were wearing out and would soon need replacement.

Case solved the problem in what seemed at the time to be an innovative manner. Looking over the company history, it seems that they were just doing what Jerome I. Case himself would have done. He would have gone to the expert and borrowed technolo-

This satisfied Case customer had three of these outfits.
A Model L tractor with a Prairie combine harvests the
wheat in Alberta, Canada. *J. I. Case Archives*

Case, Case, Case, Case. How many times can you find
the name on the machinery. This tractor-combine
team is harvesting in the wide open spaces during
1929. *J. I. Case Archives*

Your choice of 2 transmissions...

Case-o-matic DRIVE

senses the load...increases torque power

NO CLUTCHING!
NO SHIFTING!
NO STALLING!

At last, the tractor your grandmother could drive. The Case 800 series was introduced during the 1950s and came out with power steering, power shifting, disc brakes, and "Case-o-matic." It comes with all the attachments for slicing, dicing, and shredding with "living-room comfort." And no, I didn't make that one up. *J. I. Case Archives*

gy that had already been developed. And that's what Case did. They went to Cummins Diesel, the world leader in diesel engine development and design.

Case and Cummins set up a joint venture and called it the Consolidated Diesel Corporation (CDC). The program was first started in 1978 and went into production at an all-new plant in Rocky Mount, North Carolina, in 1983. It was brand spanking new, top to bottom. It has been described as the engineer's dream. The first prototype diesel was produced in 1979, and the CDC diesel is considered to be the finest engine available. It powers a wide range of Case equipment, from tractors and delivery vehicles to excavators, bulldozers, and loader backhoes. If you ever get

A Case Model L doing heavy duty pulling of a three-bottom, 14in plow. The farmer is turning sod in 1933. *J. I. Case Archives*

148

The Model L was noted for its outstanding drawing power, and here it is doing two jobs at once on the drawbar, plowing and planting. *J. I. Case Archives*

the chance, you should buy Eldon a cup of coffee and let him tell you about the time he got to sit down with a white sheet of paper.

Engineering for Florida—the Locals Know Best

Frequently, Case will make special modifications to their tractors to accommodate local conditions. The local distributors work together with Case engineering to come up with a product that meets local needs. For example, the Case dealer in Fort Ocala, Florida, made a lot of implements to go with the fruit tractor. He made a tree hook, a tree hole digger, and Case made him a special PTO shaft for the digger.

Since the soil is sandy, the farmer liked to let the weeds grow to keep the soil from blowing. Then he only cultivated around the tree base, not in the middle of the rows. When Case came out with the Model 400, they made a special modification on the orchard tractor. They took an additional 6in out of the center at his request. He needed a short tractor, so he could make shorter turns.

He made a special cutter for trimming his trees, and then he built a sprayer attachment. He was one of the first dealers to develop a local tire for his equipment. He first modified his automobile tires. He took his wheels and cut his tires down the center and put a band down the middle to spread his tires. He used to ride his car on the sand dunes. "I don't get very good

The soil conditions in the Palouse, Washington, area are legendary, and a farmer needed a tracked power unit. But he had the good sense to use a Case plow, modifying it into a six-bottom unit that got the job done. *J. I. Case Archives*

You can teach an old tractor new tricks. This one, first introduced in the '40s, is showing off a new implement, looks like a new baler. The driver is also showing off the latest in safety shoes for 1954. *J. I. Case Archives*

Tractors, the final frontier. Threshing, picking, binding—you name it. It's now a one-person operation. Big news is breaking all right, and the news is that farm production just made another quantum leap forward. *J. I. Case Archives*

tire mileage," he would say, " but I never get stuck."

When Case finally came out with the 400 diesel tractor, Case made it in an orchard tractor and sent it down to Florida for the dealer to try. "I can't sell these," he said. "They just don't sell down here." Knowing that he was an innovator, Case engineering found that extremely difficult to understand. The designers just couldn't figure out why the hot new diesels wouldn't sell in Florida. So Eldon Brumbaugh and a product engineer went down to find out why the diesels weren't selling. They drove along the Florida roads, looking at all the other tractors in the field, and all the John Deeres were diesel.

They finally drove up into Fort Ocala and quickly realized why the dealer couldn't sell diesels—he was the local LP gas distributor. He punched the cash register every time he delivered a load of low-pressure gas. Diesels would have cut into his pocketbook.

California Farmers are Different

Features that were developed for the orchard tractors in Florida were not always applicable for tractors for the citrus industry in California. Case couldn't sell a three-point hitch on the tractor in Florida, but California wanted the three-point hitch. The Californians wanted to seat the operator forward, to straddle a seat like a Ford tractor. So Case built a tractor with a special platform to straddle the transmission, just for that market. What else did Case make for the California market? Just a few local implements. Californians tended to use the regular Case machines, buying those with much bigger horsepower since their farms were so big.

Case did make a very good disc plow in Stockton, California, for western farmers. Out in the Southwest, disc plows are used by farmers, because they plow pretty deep. In some western areas they never plow less than 12in deep. By contrast, in Wisconsin, farmers rarely plow more than 6in, because the topsoil is so shallow. There are widely differing conditions across the country that change the need for implements.

Case and the Tobacco Harvester

Case did not do very much development in the design of specialized implements for local crops. Usually they let the local Case distributor make the decision about what implement would work best for a particular crop. And they let the local distributor buy any implements produced by a local manufacturer. The implement designers at corporate headquarters usually did not get involved.

There is one interesting exception. Case became involved in the development of a tobacco harvester. It had a small chassis with people sitting down below and a conveyor belt on top. The leaves of tobacco ripen at the different times. On this harvester, a person sits on the bottom and clips the lower leaves of the plant. The leaves are put on the conveyor belt, and the person on top then stacks them. It was self-contained, moving down the rows between the plants.

After World War II, Case acquired several manufacturing plants to meet their expanding markets. One of the plants was Kilby Steel Company at Anniston, Alabama. Kilby made manure spreaders, rakes, and plows for local Case distributors. Case engineering saw an opportunity to produce a tobacco harvester for this rapidly expanding crop in the southeastern United States.

Case also looked at cotton pickers but decided to buy one rather than build one themselves. The cotton pickers and cotton strippers were designed to mount on the tractor, but few sold. Efficient cotton picking today is done by a harvesting machine rather than a tractor attachment.

Another manufacturing plant Case acquired about the same time was in Stockton, California. This plant also made implements for local farmers, and the California market was a big one. The California cultivators made at Stockton were somewhat special.

Case built cultivators at two plants. They made cultivators at Rockford and Stockton, but the ones made at the Rockford, Illinois, plant were painted green, and the ones from Stockton were painted Flambeau Red. When Case did tractor testing in the field,

How to Figure Proper Size Main Drive Pulley for Belt Driven Machinery

CASE TRACTORS besides doing such traction work as plowing, hauling, road work, harvesting, seeding, discing, listing, packing, etc., may be used for a variety of belt operations, such as threshing, baling, ensilage cutting, feed grinding, husking and shredding corn, pumping water, running a saw, etc.

Proper Size Drive Pulleys Should Be Used

How economically and satisfactorily belt work may be accomplished depends more on equipping the driven machine with the proper size pulley than anything else. The driven machine should be run at its rated speed with the tractor operating at its *normal* speed. A thresher, silo filler, hay baler and all belt machines must be operated at or near some specific speed in order to do satisfactory work. This should be accomplished by fitting the machine with the proper size pulley because the tractor *must be operated at its normal speed.*

A Simple Formula

If it is desired to find the size of a pulley for a certain machine to be operated by the tractor, multiply the diameter of the tractor pulley in inches by the normal speed of the tractor pulley and divide by the speed at which the driven machine should run.

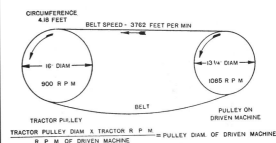

Belt Speed Chart

Example: To run a grain thresher at a cylinder speed of 1100 R. P. M. with a tractor having a 14¼-inch belt pulley that runs at 1050 R. P. M. The diameter of the separator pulley must be

$$\frac{14\frac{1}{4} \times 1050}{1100} = \text{approximately } 13\frac{1}{2} \text{ inches.}$$

(By R. P. M. is meant number of revolutions per minute).

A Simple Formula. Case emphasized engineering and targeted some of its sales literature to farmers who had been to agricultural school—or sent their children to agricultural school. This little pulley problem is from World War I vintage sales literature. *J. I. Case Archives*

The transmission on the Model L and the smaller C was relatively simple; two hardened steel roller chains running in a continuous bath of lubricating oil. *J. I. Case Archives*

the operators always tried to find a Stockton cultivator to pull. Most test crops were very green, and the orange cultivator really stood out against the crop. So the Flambeau Red, Stockton-built cultivator was always a lot more popular in corn country than the green one made in Rockford.

Case-IH in the Twenty-First Century

The agricultural machinery manufacturing business has always been volatile. A century ago there were more than two hundred manufacturers turning out one or two types of tractor; now there seems to be just one or two companies building two hundred kinds of equipment. Sometimes we think that things only happen quickly in the present, because our global electronics systems make us aware how quickly things happen.

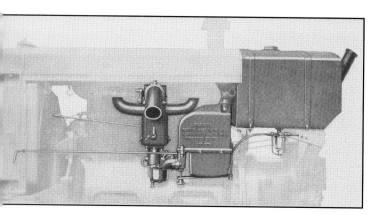

Like the transmission, the fuel system was as simple and efficient as the engineers could make it. It used either gasoline or kerosene and had filters which could be cleaned easily, an important feature in dusty field work. *J. I. Case Archives*

But even a century ago, changes in technology could put a company or an industry out of business in just a few months. So what does the future hold for ag machinery builders?

Tractor builders, like auto makers and other equipment manufacturers, are reducing the number of their employees as robotics and telecommunications networks make their businesses more efficient. It's called "downsizing," and it's part of an overall worldwide trend. In some instances, the downsizing has resulted in bitter disputes with labor unions, hampering corporate viability and destroying goodwill. Some corporations will disappear as a result of prolonged strikes. Buyouts and mergers are always part of the business game. Can Case manage to survive in the global economy?

We feel confident that Case-IH will be around for quite a while. A few things don't change—people still need to eat. And Case has been an international presence for more than a century. It's interesting to remember that Case was one of the earliest American steam traction engine builders in Russia, sending threshers and steam engines as early as 1902, just after the turn of the century. At the same time, Case was also sending agricultural machines to Brazil and other parts of South America.

Will Case-IH expand its traditional markets in Europe and South America in the next century? What about the Asian markets? In the 1990s, *Fortune* magazine once again identified the Case loader backhoe as one of the "100 Products that America Makes Best." Will American ag products continue to lead the world, or will it be American designed and engineered, but built overseas? Or will other global machinery manufacturing giants serve international farm markets?

Knowing that many farmers liked to do the routine maintenance on their tractors, Case built a radiator that was easy to clean. *J. I. Case Archives*

Positive ignition—another giant leap forward. No more dislocated thumbs, sore shoulders, or broken arms from hand-cranking. *J. I. Case Archives*

Our growing world needs food and people to grow it. And technology has not yet figured out a way to control the weather, so there will always be a need to feed a starving population somewhere on our globe. We feel confident that Case-IH managers and employees have the values, attitudes, and flexibility to meet the challenges of the twenty-first century.

Mr. Quality Control, Retiree Harry Kline

When you have a crazy technical question about any kind of Case equipment, from determining the correct paint colors on "Old Abe" to outlining the finer points of boiler repair, you may end up being referred to former Case company employee, Harry Kline. He's been retired for a while, but he is such an important technical resource that his phone number stays in the engineering Rolodexes.

A favorite story about Harry is very reminiscent of a similar story of J. I. Case and the defective thresher that Case himself finally set on fire back in 1884. Harry has had a number of assignments at Case over the years: sales engineer, product engineer, sales manager, quality control manager—but they all mean about the same thing. If there was a really tough engineering problem, Harry got tapped to go out and fix it.

All that experience means that Harry could spot defective equipment on the assembly line. So one day when Harry marked a large expensive hunk of Case hardware for the scrap pile, he thought he had the situation resolved. A couple of days later, he was making his rounds on the line, and he recognized the same defective machine.

So Harry called the foreman over and once again had the junker sidelined, designated for recycling. To his surprise and disgust, he found the machine back on the line some time later. Harry didn't hesitate. He was not going to let a patched-up, substandard piece of equipment go to the customer. He grabbed a torch and neatly quartered it. J. I. Case would have been proud of him.

MILESTONES IN HISTORY

The success and growth of the Case corporation depended on a great many related factors in American agricultural development. The eventual success of the gasoline tractor, for example, was dependent on gasoline refining and the growth of a retail distribution network for petroleum products.

The wide and rapid spread of thresher usage was related to the development of the many American railroads; these heavy machines were delivered to farms by railroad. And, of course, farmers are especially vulnerable to bad weather and pests as well as general economic events such as wars and financial depressions. A few historic milestones important to the Case corporation are listed below.

1819—Jerome Increase Case is born in the Williamstown district of New York state. He was the fourth of seven children: four boys, then three girls.

1825—Erie Canal opens connecting New York with Buffalo and the Great Lakes. The vast plains of the Midwest are now accessible for agricultural development.

1836—Wisconsin Territory established.

1842—J. I. Case heads West with six ground hog threshers; sets up business in Rochester, Wisconsin.

1844—Case demonstrates a prototype thresher-separator of his own design and manufacture. He moves to nearby Racine and builds his factory.

1848—Wisconsin becomes a state, and Racine is incorporated as a city.

1857—Major economic "panic" strikes the United States.

1859—The first oil well in America is drilled in western Pennsylvania by E. L. Drake.

1861—The Civil War begins. Thousands of Wisconsin farmers go off to war, leaving fewer workers to grow more crops for the war effort.

The Eighth Wisconsin Regiment, Company C, adopts an eagle as their mascot and names him "Old Abe," after the president.

1862—The Homestead Act is signed; farmers can now file claims on open lands and establish homesteads of 160 acres per person.

1863—Jerome Case forms the J. I. Case Company with three partners; Massena Erskine, Robert Baker, and Stephen Bull.

1865—The Civil War comes to a close.

1869—The Central Pacific and Western Pacific railroads meet at Promontory Point, Utah. Railroads are now able to deliver threshing machines and other large agricultural implements across the West to California by train.

Case begins work on a steam traction engine, and "Old No. 1" makes its debut. (Old No. 1 is now on display at the Smithsonian.)

1876—Case exhibits an Eclipse thresher at the Philadelphia Centennial Exhibition.

Case introduces its first self-propelled steam traction engine. The engine can move on its own but needs horses for steering.

1878—The Paris World's Fair; Case first appears in international competitions.

N. A. Otto exhibits a gasoline-powered engine at the same Paris Exposition.

1880—J. I. Case buys his famous "pacer," Jay Eye Cee.

J. I. Case and Company is dissolved, and the J. I. Case Threshing Machine Company is incorporated.

1884—Case develops a steering device for the steam traction machine.

1885—The Case Company signs an agreement with W. R. Grace to market Case threshers in South America.

1891—Case builds a steam plow for Californian Jacob Price.

1891—J. I. Case dies at Racine, Wisconsin, from the complications of diabetes, at age seventy-three.

1892—California inventor James Paterson develops and tests a gasoline traction engine for the Case directors, but the company declines to put it in production.

1893–1897—Worldwide depression puts all business in decline. J. I. Case Threshing Machine Company reorganizes and hangs on; so does the J. I. Case Plow Works.

1894—The Case trademark eagle "Old Abe" takes his place on the world globe. The J. I. Case Company would maintain this design for more than seventy-five years.

1895—Case begins selling several sizes of two-cylinder gasoline motors.

1898—Branch houses developed to sell, distribute, and service equipment manufactured by Case.

Rudolf Diesel introduces a really successful working model of the diesel engine.

1900—Rapid development of crude-oil pipeline networks following the discovery of oil in Texas, Kansas, and Oklahoma.

1902—The International-Harvester Company is created by combining several firms.

1904—The all-steel thresher makes its appearance. It was lighter and more durable than wood and was extremely successful.

1905—Case produces an automatic baler.

1906—International-Harvester produces a gasoline tractor.

Case opens a materials laboratory to test parts from contractors and suppliers.

1907—Henry Ford successfully tests a prototype tractor, but his board of directors refuses to put it into production.

1910—The expression *Power Farming* enters the American farm vocabulary.

The 30-60 and the 20-40 tractors appear on the market and are entered in competition in 1912.

1910—Case expands equipment lines and markets dump wagons made at the Troy Wagon Works. They also distribute gasoline engines under license from the Raymond Company and road graders and scrapers from the Perfection Road Machinery Company in Galion, Ohio. Corn shellers and huskers are added to the line.

1911—The 30-60 traction engine goes to Winnipeg and brings home a gold medal.

1912 to about 1927—Case makes and races automobiles—a roadster, coupe, and sedan.

1914—The Sattley plow is introduced and sold by Case.

1915—The 10-20 is introduced, the first Case tractor with a "tricycle" wheel in front. Tillage equipment manufactured by Grand Detour is added to the catalog.

1917—Henry Ford finally starts a new company to build tractors; his Fordson joins the competition.

1918—Plow maker John Deere buys the Waterloo Tractor Company and joins the tractor business.

1919—Case acquires the Grand Detour Plow Company which offers a complete line of plows and tillage equipment.

Solid rubber tires become available for tractors.

A major improvement in gasoline refining takes place with development of an improved process involving catalytic cracking.

1920—The Nebraska Tractor Tests begin. Case is an early and active participant in the tractor trials.

Case offers rubber tires on its 10-18 and 15-27 models.

1923—The color scheme for Case tractors is changed from hunter green to a light gray.

John Deere introduces the Model D, a two-cylinder model designed to sell for about $1,000, at the encouragement of Deere board member Leon Clausen. The next year, Leon Clausen is hired as the new president of J. I. Case.

The one hundred thousandth thresher comes off the line.

1928—The corporate name is changed again. It is now officially the J. I. Case Company.

Case acquires the Emerson-Brantingham Farm Equipment Company. Case now owns a complete implement line which includes manure spreaders, seed drills, cultivators, side delivery rakes, binders, and an additional tractor line.

1929—Wall Street crashes, and the Great Depression forces many tractor manufacturers to close.

Case introduces a new series of tractors with unit-frame construction; the Model L is followed closely by a Model C and then the Model CC, a cultivator.

A power take-off (PTO) mounted at the rear is offered on the Model L.

Case not only survives the Depression but expands substantially. By cutting salaries, reducing inventory, and living on substantial cash reserves banked in the previous decade, Case maintains a leadership position.

1931—Caterpillar introduces the Model 65 with a diesel engine. The competition sits up.

1932—Case brings out eight combines in three sizes. They also debut a one-man combine with a PTO and a corn picker.

1933—Case considers adding a diesel engine to its tractor line-up but abandons production plans after several years of prototype testing.

1934—Case offers rubber tires with Case-made wheels.

1935—Case brings out the Model R, the first general purpose small tractor in the Case line.

Case introduces the Motor Lift, a mechanical implement lifter powered by the PTO. This allows plows to be lifted at the end of the rows or wherever a snag is encountered.

1939—Case debuts a new series of tractors, their all time best sellers painted Flambeau Red, a signature color for a decade.

A few limited-use tractors are offered to satisfy some specialized farmers—the tobacco harvester, for example.

1940—World War II begins in Europe, and Case introduces the V for Victory series tractors. Made of parts from other manufacturers, the series is replaced by VAs in 1942.

1941—The Japanese bomb Peal Harbor.

Case is heavily involved in the war effort but finds a shortage of material for its own continuing tractor production.

1945—The second World War comes to a close, and Case is involved in a nasty 440-day labor strike. Case has difficulty catching up with the other tractor builders.

1947—The Marshall Plan opens up new markets for farm machinery in Europe.

1948—Ford introduces Model 8N without crediting inventor Harry Ferguson for his revolutionary three-point hitch. Litigation between Ford and Ferguson dragged on until 1952.

1949—Case introduces their Eagle Hitch—an improvement on the three-point system first introduced by Ferguson. The new Case hitch is featured on the VA models.

Hydraulic controls replace the motor-lift system.

1951—Liquid propane gas (LPG) is available for farm equipment.

1952—Live PTO added to SC and DC tractors.

1953—The new 400 and 500 series tractors debut with a diesel tractor offered in the 500 series. This tractor is heralded as the finest diesel available.

Thresher production finally closes.

1954—The "disposable" plow is introduced.

1957—Case-O-Matic drive is introduced. Tractors now have all the amenities.

1964—The Case Company is acquired by the Kern County Land Company of San Francisco.

The Traction King is introduced. It's a turbocharged diesel with four-wheel steering, developed with the Clarke Forklift Company for large acreage agricultural operations.

1965—Comfort Kings

1967—Case is acquired by Tenneco Incorporated of Houston, Texas.

1969—Old Abe trademark is finally retired, replaced by a new, contemporary logo.

Agri Kings, four-wheel-drive machines with fully enclosed cabs, are introduced. The Agri King Model 1470 is the largest agricultural tractor ever made by Case.

1978—Case forms a joint venture with Cummins Diesel called the Consolidated Diesel Corporation to develop and manufacture an engine specifically for agricultural applications.

1985—Parent company Tenneco, Inc., acquires International Harvester and merges the agricultural line with Case.

A new color scheme is adopted, Harvester Red and Case Black.

1990—Case suffers through several years of corporate downsizing and layoffs due to poor business economy worldwide.

1992—Case celebrates its 150th anniversary as a corporation.

And A Quick Look at the Tractor Line-Up

Case-IH continues to design, develop, and manufacture tractors and a wide assortment of related implements and agricultural equipment. The following lists emphasize what current historians call "The Golden Age of the Tractor," the machines built and sold by Case before about 1955. The dates shown are the dates the tractors were built. This list was compiled from production information in the appendix of the Case history written by Dave Erb and Eldon Brumbaugh, *Full Steam Ahead, Volume 1*.

Some branch houses and distributors had a few models in their back rooms years after a new series had been introduced. That's because they sold better that way to the more conservative farmers. Some customers just didn't want to be stampeded into buying one of those new-fangled, overpriced showroom models with all the fancy expensive extras like rubber tires and headlights.

1876–1924—Steam Traction

Case manufactured steam traction equipment, nearly 36,000 steam tractors in nearly fifty years of production. Surprisingly, the years of the greatest numbers of steam tractors produced are between 1900 and 1915, overlapping the beginnings of the gasoline tractor.

1911 — The Gasoline Tractors

Model	Description	Years Built	Quantity
30-60	Otherwise known as the famous Model 60. A Winnipeg Winner, looks like a steamer. Reportedly only five survive.	1911-1916	525
20-40	The other Winnipeg Winner, also looks like a steamer, but a third smaller.	1912-1919	4,303
12-25	This looks like a real tractor; it has a low profile and open platform for the driver.	1913-1918	3,351
10-20	This tricycle version showed up to compete with "The Bull." It was the first Case tractor with a four-cylinder engine.	1915-1918	6,679

1917 — The Crossmotors

Model	Description	Years Built	Quantity
9-18	Considered the first in the series of the "crossmounts," replaced by a modified 10-18.	1916-1920	6,687
10-18	The first Case tractor with a one-piece cast iron frame; also came with solid rubber tires. Wallis Cub may have been inspiration.	1917-1920	7,367
12-20	Not much bigger than the 10-18, but a good replacement; weighs a petite two tons.	1921-1927	9,237
15-27	Beefier all around than the 12-20 and a ton heavier.	1919-1924	17,629
18-32	Priced at $1,350 and not as popular as the 15-27 it was supposed to replace.	1925-1928	9,890
22-40	For large farms, pulls 5 plows.	1919-1924	1,757
25-45	The most expensive tractor in the series, cost over $3,000.	1925-1928	1,184
40-72	The BIG one, more tractor than most farmers wanted. Really suited for road building. Weighed in at nearly ten tons!	1920-1923	only 42

1928 — Standards and Row Crops

Model	Description	Years Built	Quantity
Series L	Produced until 1940; few models.		
Model L	A totally new design; this is the tractor that established Case's reputation as a tractor builder.	1929-1940	31,871
Model LI	The industrial version, also included a military version.	1929-1940	2,196
Series C			
Model C	A smaller row crop version of the L.	1929-1939	20,478
Model CC	A cultivator; two-speed transmission offered.	1929-1939	29,824
Model CI	Industrial version for warehouse uses.	1929-1940	791
Model CO	Orchard use—small orchards.	1929-1938	1,275
Model CO-VS	Designed just for vineyard.	Built four years	190
Model CCS	Also a rare tractor, designed for sugar cane plantations.	1937-1938	115
Model CH	Peter LeTourneau says this is the rarest of the rare.	1937 only	7
Series R			
Model RC	The row crop, first offered in 1935, the plain vanilla R came later. This is just to confuse a Case enthusiast who thinks he has the model sequence straight.	1935-1939	15,948
Model R	Important transition tractor with Flambeau paint and new grille, old engineering.	1938-1939	

1939	The Flambeaus (also known as "The Classics")		
Model	**Description**	**Years Built**	**Quantity**
Series D	Produced from 1939 to 1953.		
Model D			
Model DC3	By a wide margin, the most popular D.		54,925
Model DC4			14,016
Model DH	Built two years only; Hasselman diesel engines offered.	1939-1940	141
Model DO	The orchard version.		2,874
Model DV	Vineyard model, spotty production.		582
Model DI	Two wheel widths; only 445 narrow treads built.		8,548
Model DCS	The sugar cane model.		
Series S			
Model S			8,390
Model SC	The row crop.	1941-1954	58,991
Model SO	Orchard and grove tractor.	1941-1952	1,817
Model SI	Industrial.	1942-1952	3,740
Model Sex	Extendible wheels.	1941-1952	3,627
Model SOEx	The orchard tractor with extendible wheels.	1941, 1947, 1949-1952	70
Series L	Produced 1940–1952.		
Model LA	Replaced the Big L.	1940-1952	35,493
Model LAI	The industrial one.	1941-1952	6,125
Model LAIH	The Hasselman diesel.	1943	23 only
Model LAI	Industrial.	1941-1952	6,125
Model LA			
Series V	Vee for Victory, the wartime tractors. Built for two years.		
Model V	Made from outside parts, a Continental engine and a Clark transmission.	1940-1942	2,321
Model VC	The cultivator.	1940-1942	12,462
Model VI	Only a handful of homely little machines.	1941-1942	734
Model VO		1941-1942	511
Series VA	Replaces V Series.		
Model VA	1942.	1942-1953	17,583
Model VAC	The Eagle Hitch came out on the 1950 models.		94,267
Model VAC-14		1953-1955	7,505
Model VAI		1942-1955	15,033
Model VAO	Also VAO-15.	1942-1955	6,326
Model VAH		1947-1955	2,016
Model VAS		1951-1954	1,559
Model VAIW		1944-1953	3,793
The Numbers			
Model 300	Replaces old S Series, painted beige with red trim.	1955	
Model 400	All new! Engine and tranny both.	1953	
Model 500	Finally...a DIESEL, but it's the last Flambeau	1953-1955	5,225

BIBLIOGRAPHY

The CASE Books

Brumbaugh, Eldon, and Dave Erb. *Full Steam Ahead: J. I. Case, Tractors and Equipment 1842-1955.* St. Joseph, Michigan: American Society of Agricultural Engineers, 1993.

Holmes, Michael S. *J. I. Case, The First 150 Years.* Racine, Wisconsin: The Case Corporation, 1992. The official history of the company, commissioned to celebrate the anniversary of 150 years as a corporation.

Leffingwell, Randy. *The American Farm Tractor.* Osceola, Wisconsin: Motorbooks International, 1991.

LeTourneau, Peter. *Illustrated CASE Tractor Buyer's Guide.* Osceola, Wisconsin: Motorbooks International, 1994.

Wendel, C. H. *150 Years of J. I. Case.* Sarasota, Florida: Crestline Publishing Company, 1991.

Archival Resources from the Case corporate archive. Booklets, catalogs, flyers, and pamphlets from the extensive collection at the Case archives in Racine, Wisconsin.

Other Books Used for Reference

Ardrey, Robert L. *American Agricultural Implements*, New York, New York: ARNO Press, 1972. A reprint edition of the 1894 book, subtitled "A review of Invention and Development in the Agricultural Implement Industry of the United States." Offered in two parts. Originally printed in Chicago.

Johnson, Paul C. *Farm Inventions in the Making of America.* Des Moines, Iowa: Wallace-Homestead Book Company, 1976. A pictorial history of farm machinery featuring engravings from old farm magazines and books.

Pile, John. *Dictionary of 20th Century Design.* New York, New York: Roundtable Press, Inc., 1990.

Williams, Robert C. *Fordson, Farmall, and Poppin' Johnny; A History of the Farm Tractor and Its Impact on America.* Urbana and Chicago, Illinois: University of Illinois Press, 1987. An interesting look at the competition.

INDEX